T0165197

LEGAL CONSUMER TIPS AND SECRETS

Also by Charles Jerome Ware

Understanding the Law: A Primer

The Immigration Paradox: 15 Tips for Winning Immigration Cases

Charles Jerome Ware

http://charlesware.blogspot.com/

http://thelawyersmailbox.blogspot.com/

http://twitter.com/CharlesJWare

http://open.salon.com/blog/charlesjware

LEGAL CONSUMER TIPS AND SECRETS

Avoiding Debtors' Prison in the United States

by

Charles Jerome Ware

www.charlesjeromeware.com

Former Special Counsel to the Chairman of the
United States Federal Trade Commission

iUniverse, Inc.
Bloomington

Legal Consumer Tips and Secrets
Avoiding Debtors' Prison in the United States

Copyright © 2011 by Charles Jerome Ware.

All rights reserved. No part of this book may be used or reproduced by any means, graphic, electronic, or mechanical, including photocopying, recording, taping or by any information storage retrieval system without the written permission of the publisher except in the case of brief quotations embodied in critical articles and reviews.

The information, ideas, and suggestions in this book are not intended to render legal advice. Before following any suggestions contained in this book, you should consult your personal attorney. Neither the author nor the publisher shall be liable or responsible for any loss or damage allegedly arising as a consequence of your use or application of any information or suggestions in this book.

iUniverse books may be ordered through booksellers or by contacting:

iUniverse
1663 Liberty Drive
Bloomington, IN 47403
www.iuniverse.com
1-800-Authors (1-800-288-4677)

Because of the dynamic nature of the Internet, any web addresses or links contained in this book may have changed since publication and may no longer be valid. The views expressed in this work are solely those of the author and do not necessarily reflect the views of the publisher, and the publisher hereby disclaims any responsibility for them.

Any people depicted in stock imagery provided by Thinkstock are models, and such images are being used for illustrative purposes only.
Certain stock imagery © Thinkstock.

ISBN: 978-1-4620-5182-3 (sc)
ISBN: 978-1-4620-5184-7 (hc)
ISBN: 978-1-4620-5183-0 (ebk)

Printed in the United States of America

iUniverse rev. date: 09/16/2011

GENERAL
TABLE OF CONTENTS

PART III: SUMMARY:
LEGAL CONSUMER TIPS AND SECRETS

DETAILED
TABLE OF CONTENTS

CHAPTER FOUR: FIFTEEN (15) TIPS
FOR AVOIDING FORECLOSURE

CHAPTER FIVE: AVOIDING IDENTITY THEFT
AND IDENTITY FRAUD

CHAPTER SIX: WORK-AT-HOME SCAMS
AND SCHEMES [EMPLOYMENT]

CHAPTER SEVEN: FROM CHARLES PONZI
TO BERNARD MADOFF: THE "PONZI" AND
OTHER INVESTMENT SCHEMES

CHAPTER EIGHT: THE AFFINITY SCAM

CHAPTER NINE: FOUR (4) THINGS NOT TO DO WHEN YOU ARE IN DEBT

CHAPTER TEN: AVOIDING DEBT SETTLEMENT SCAMS

CHAPTER ELEVEN: THE "NIGERIAN," THE "SINGAPORE," THE "IRISH LOTTERY," AND OTHER INTERNET SCAMS

CHAPTER TWELVE: HOME IMPROVEMENT CONSUMER SECRETS AND TIPS

CHAPTER SIXTEEN:
SECRETS AND TIPS FOR AVOIDING
DEBT COLLECTION HARASSMENT

CHAPTER SEVENTEEN:
RECOGNIZING AND AVOIDING
TAX DEBT SETTLEMENT SCAMS

CHAPTER EIGHTEEN:
DEALING WITH GOVERNMENT AGENCIES

CHAPTER NINETEEN: AVOIDING DEBTORS' PRISON IN THE UNITED STATES

CHAPTER TWENTY: CONCLUDING THOUGHTS

PART III: SUMMARY: LEGAL CONSUMER TIPS AND SECRETS

SUMMARY: LEGAL CONSUMER TIPS AND SECRETS
—Avoiding Debtors' Prison In The United States—

Dedicated to my family, friends, clients and readers.

Attorney's Note

The old Latin warning "Caveat emptor" (Let the buyer beware) appears to be making a comeback in our Society—

Charles Jerome Ware
Former Special Counsel to the Chairman of the
United States Federal Trade Commission

Consumerism is now the "biggest religion" in the United States; surpassing Evangelicals, Protestants, and Catholics [Chapter 20].

Consumers in America and throughout the world today, more than ever, must be educated, informed and aware when purchasing their goods and services.

As examples, the consumer should know:

A limited warranty on a product is not a waiver of liability for the product's harm to the consumer [Chapter 1, "Personal Injury 101"].

Only about one in 5 medical malpractice claims against doctors results in a monetary payout or some other settlement to the claimant. This is the case even though about one in 14 doctors has a malpractice claim filed against them each year. In other words, it is much easier to file a medical malpractice claim than it is to win one [Chapter 2, "Medical Malpractice 101].

"Debtors' Prison" (debtors' imprisonment) exists today in the United States. That's right . . . you can go to jail in the United States today (in the year 2011) over a debt owed, even though you have not committed a crime [Chapter 19, "Avoiding Debtors' Prison in the United States"].

More than a third of all states in America permit incarceration of borrowers or debtors who cannot or do not pay their debts. In a survey of 20 judges across the U.S., the pattern has developed that the number of borrowers threatened with arrest by judges in courtrooms has substantially increased in recent years [Chapter 19].

"Produce the note!" is probably the most important phrase or statement a homeowner can make when facing foreclosure on his or her home [Chapter 4, "Fifteen (15) Tips for Avoiding Foreclosure"]. It is no less than remarkable how many times your promissory note on the property can be misfiled, made unavailable temporarily, or even lost between the transfer of your housenote from one creditor (mortgagor) to another.

Bankruptcy versus Foreclosure: Which looks better on your credit report? It depends on the homeowner's specific circumstances. Usually, a foreclosure remains on the homeowner's credit report for 7 years, and a bankruptcy will remain for 10 years [Chapter 4].

Credit Collection is legalized invasion of privacy [Chapter 3, "Credit Bureau, Credit Scores and the Credit Business"]. The collection of consumers' personal credit information, the processing and storage of this personal credit information, and the selling of the consumers' personal information is a multi-billion dollar business annually!

Credit reports are frequently wrong . . . and, they are biased against the consumer [Chapter 3]. In contrast to the general public impression, credit bureaus are typically <u>not</u> taxpayer-funded government agencies. On the contrary, credit bureaus are routinely private, high profit-making companies that collect, "process" in complete secrecy, and <u>sell</u> the consumers' personal information or credit history for huge profits.

The consumer has the <u>right</u> to know what is in his or her credit report or credit file; and he or she should exercise that right at a minimum of once or twice a year. In many cases, the consumer can qualify to get a copy of the report for free [*Chapter 3*].

In general, **credit cards** probably should be treated as your enemy; not your friend [Chapter 3].

For American credit card holders, the average credit card debt amount per holder has been estimated by some authorities to be $15,788.00 [Chapter 9, "Four (4) Things Not To Do When You Are In Debt"].

It has been guesstimated by some experts that it would take more than 40 years for the average consumer to pay off most credit cards by making just minimum payments [Chapter 9].

BEWARE of any internet solicitation that uses language such as:

— "God IS GOOD!"
— "Can You Work With Me?"
— "Congratulations!!! You have won!", etc.

Experience shows that internet solicitations that begin with, or include early in the message, these types of messages (or language) are highly suspect in terms of their legitimacy. They are frequently "Nigerian" scams or schemes (Chapter 11, ". . . Internet Scams"). Everyone is a potential target of scammers.

REMEMBER the wisdom of contracts: the BOLD (large) print in a Contract giveth, and the Fine (small) print taketh away: This point is virtually a universal truth (Chapter 15, "Contract Law for the Consumer").

AVOID, if at all possible, signing any contract that contains a "confessed judgment" clause. This clause is very dangerous legally and financially for the consumer, and it is usually "slipped into" the contract or agreement by the creditor (Chapter 15, "Contract Law for the Consumer").

Despite threats from unscrupulous bill collectors, there are many types of income that the consumer debtor may have that cannot be attached, liened against, or garnished by creditors. For example, many Federal benefits are exempt from garnishment; including

(1) Social Security benefits, (2) Veteran's benefits, (3) Civil Service and Federal Retirement and Disability benefits, (4) Armed Service members' pay, (5) Military Annuities and Survivors' Benefits, (6) Student Assistance income, (7) Railroad Retirement Benefits, (8) Merchant Seamen Wages, (9) Longshoremen's and Harbor Workers' Death and Disability Benefits, (10) Foreign Service Retirement and Disability Benefits, (11) Federal Emergency Management Agency Federal Disaster Assistance, and (12) Compensation for Injury, Death, or Detention of Employees of U.S. Contractors Outside the United States [Chapter 16, "Secrets and Tips for Avoiding Debt Collection Harassment"].

In truth, in the vast majority of cases, what so-called "tax debt settlement" companies or specialists are actually selling the tax debt client is the service of representing the tax debtor in the Internal Revenue Service's (IRS's) "Offer in Compromise (OIC)" process. This established IRS "Offer in Compromise (OIC)" process is legitimate, but the average taxpayer's chances of getting the relief they want or expect, or even promised by the so-called "tax specialist", is remote [Chapter 17, "Recognizing and Avoiding Tax Debt Settlement Scams"].

As with all of my books and other publications, including **Understanding the Law: A Primer** (2008), and **The Immigration Paradox: Fifteen (15) Tips for Winning Immigration Cases**, (2009), this book is written specifically to help and assist the reader.

This book, **Legal Consumer Tips and Secrets**, is intended and designed to provide valuable insight and information for the consumer. The reader is specifically and particularly advised to consult a qualified attorney or other professional for specific answers to specific consumer and legal questions.

The information provided in this book is not legal or consumer advice, but is general information on some legal and consumer issues which may be commonly encountered. The reader is strongly advised to seek expert or competent advice and consultation to answer specific questions and address specific issues.

Thanks to manuscriptist Linda Gail Brown Smith as well as Shakespearean actor and teacher Jamie Jager for their valuable assistance with this book.

I hope this book will be of assistance, help and value to the reader.

PART I

PHYSICAL HARM

Chapter One

Personal Injury 101

He sure had me worried.

> In a terrible accident one night at a railroad crossing, a train smashed into a car and pushed it nearly four hundred yards down the track. Though no one was killed, the driver of the car took the train company to court since he had suffered a personal injury.
>
> At the trial, the engineer insisted that he had given the driver ample warning by waving his lantern back and forth for nearly a minute. He even stood and convincingly demonstrated how he'd done it. The court believed his story, and the personal injury lawsuit was dismissed.
>
> "Congratulations," the lawyer said to the engineer when it was over. "You did superbly under cross-examination."
>
> "Thanks," he said, "but he sure had me worried."
>
> "How's that?" the lawyer asked.
>
> "I was afraid he was going to ask if the lantern was lit!"

By definition, "personal injury law" is that area of the law designed to protect you—your body, mind and emotions—because of somebody else's act or failure to act. It is also known as "tort law." In a successful personal injury or tort action, the person who caused the injury or harm is called upon to compensate the person who suffered the losses. Generally, there are three established theories of personal injury or tort liability: negligence, strict liability and intentional misconduct.

The most common typical kinds of personal injury claims include traffic accidents, so-called "slip and falls", tripping accidents, accidents at work, assault and battery claims, accidents in the home, product defects or so-called product liability claims, *inter alia*. On a broader scale, "personal injury" can also include medical malpractice, dental malpractice, orthopedic (chiropractic) malpractice, and the category of *industrial disease* cases which encompass asbestosis and mesothelioma, emphysema, pneumoconiosis, silicosis, chronic bronchitis, asthma, chronic obstructive pulmonary disease and chronic obstructive airways disease, vibration white finger, occupational deafness, occupational stress, contact dermatitis, sarcodosis, post-traumatic stress syndrome (PTSS), and repetitive strain injury ["Nolo's Free Dictionary of Law Terms and Legal Definitions", Nolo.com, September 18, 2009; Black's Law Dictionary; Barron's Law Dictionary].

My main tip for the reader in this chapter on personal injury is that too many consumers who are victims of personal injury settle their cases too soon; without full and proper medical treatment and physical rehabilitation.

Negligence occurs when a person's conduct falls below a legally recognized standard of taking reasonable care under the circumstances to protect others from harm. Persons who act negligently do not intend to cause an accident that injures another person. Instead, their liability develops from careless or thoughtless conduct or a failure to act when a reasonable person under the circumstances would have acted. Negligence is the basis for liability in the majority of personal injury lawsuits, including automobile accidents and medical malpractice.

In the area of **strict liability**, designers and manufacturers are held strictly liable for injuries caused by their defective products. In strict liability cases, the injured person does not have to establish negligence by the user of the product. Instead, what the injured person needs to show is that the defective product was designed or manufactured in a manner that made it unreasonably dangerous or unsafe when used as intended. Strict liability is an important and growing area of tort law. It is, in effect, "liability without fault." [see, "strict liability", Barron's Law Dictionary & Black's Law Dictionary].

Intentional Misconduct claims are intentional personal injury to someone else, and "automobile accidents" are the areas in which the majority of personal injury actions arise. Automobile accidents provide a good example of how the tort system works. For example, a person has a negligence claim in a "fault" state (such as Maryland) when he or she is injured by a driver who failed to exercise reasonable care, because drivers have a duty to exercise reasonable care any time they are on the road. When drivers breach that duty and injury results to another, personal injury law, or tort law, says the injured person can recoup his or her losses. (Remember, though, the system may be very different in states that have passed "no-fault" laws.)

Intentional Misconduct claims of personal injury or tort liability must allege and prove more than just careless actions by another person. It must be alleged and proved that the offending person intended to engage in the offending conduct that he or she engaged in. From this conduct, the law infers and concludes that the offending person intended the consequences of his or her action. Further, in contrast to the negligence theory of liability for personal injury, the plaintiff (alleged victim) alleging an intentional tort does not need to show actual damages to recover. It is important to note that while perpetrators of some intentional torts—such as assault and battery, for example—can be held *criminally* liable for their actions, a tort or personal injury case is a *civil* proceeding in court brought by an individual or entity and remains totally separate from any criminal charges brought by the government.

Generally, **civil** law in the United States involves private lawsuits between two or more parties or persons, Personal injury and business disputes are just two examples. **Criminal** law involves what are considered offenses or crimes against the government. In most criminal matters, it is possible for parties or persons to go to jail or become incarcerated. It is exceedingly rare for parties or persons to go to jail in civil disputes in the United States [see, *Understanding the Law: A Primer,* by Attorney Charles Jerome Ware, Chap. 12 (Criminal Defense Practice), iUniverse Publishers (2008); and, *Law Info*, "criminal versus civil", www.lawinfo.com].

Automobiles are at the center of more lawsuits in the United States than anything else, and "automobile accidents" is the area in which the majority of personal injury actions arise.

According to the U.S. Centers for Disease Control and Prevention, in the year 2000 the estimated economic cost of motor vehicle collisions (MVCs), or "car accidents," was about $230 billion [Centers for Disease Control (CDC), www.cdc.gov/motorvehiclesafety (2011)].

Every personal injury or tort claim—regardless of whether its basis is negligence, strict liability or intentional misconduct—has two basic issues: (1) liability and (2) damages. First, was the defendant liable for the damages you suffered? Second, if so, what is the nature and extent of the damages you suffered? If you can prove liability and damages, you are in the money; our American system of justice will award you compensation for your losses.

Some often-asked questions about personal injury, also with answers, are as follows:

1. *Question*: *How do you know if you have a personal injury case?*

Answer: It's simple. First, you must have suffered an injury to your person or property. Second, your injury must be the result of someone else's fault. Third, the injury must be the result of someone's <u>unlawful</u> action. Fourth, consult an attorney for verification.

2. *Question: What kind of legal fees should I expect to pay in a personal injury case?*

Answer: Personal injury lawyers generally charge their clients on a contingent fee basis. That means you pay your lawyer only if you win. You'll sign what is called a retainer agreement with the lawyer you choose to represent you, clarifying all fees and charges. Remember that even if you lose the case, you are likely to have to pay the expenses of investigating and litigating your case, such as court filing fees and payments to investigators, court reporters and medical experts, as well as the expenses of securing medical records and reports.

3. *Question: Does a personal injury lawsuit have to be filed within a certain amount or period of time?*

Answer: Yes. Each state has certain time limits called "statute of limitations," that govern the period during which you must file a personal injury lawsuit. Here in Maryland, that period generally is within three years of the date of the injury. If you miss the statutory deadline for filing a case, your case in all likelihood will be thrown out of court. Therefore, it is very important that you speak with a lawyer as soon as you receive or discover a personal injury.

In many cases, injured parties under the age of eighteen at the time of their injuries or accidents have until the day before their twenty-first birthday to start legal proceedings for compensation. Most courts have the discretion to extend or waive the limitation period if it is considered fair and just to do so. Another limitations exception is if the bodily injury is caused by accident, the three year or so limitations period can start from the date or point when the injured party knew or should have known that he or she had a claim [see, s. 33 Limitation Act 1980; Richard Beaman, "The Three Year Limitation of Claim," Douglas Wemyss Solicitors (Leicester), October 14, 2010].

4. *Question: What if I get injured on the job?*

Answer: In addition to the already discussed personal injury or tort laws, worker's compensation laws may apply to your on-the-job injuries. Worker's compensation laws, currently in place in all 50 states and the District of Columbia, cover most workers injured on the job. Under these laws, employers compensate you for your injuries, including medical expenses, lost wages (temporary disability) and permanent or temporary disability, regardless of who is at fault. All you have to do is file notice with your employer and a claim with the state's workers' compensation commission or board [see, "Workers' Compensation", infra].

5. *Question: What is medical malpractice?*

Answer: Medical malpractice is negligence committed by a professional healthcare provider—a doctor, nurse, dentist, technician, hospital or hospital worker—whose performance of duties departs from a standard of practice of those with similar training and experience, resulting in harm to a patient or patients.

6. *Question: What do I do if I think I have a medical malpractice claim?*

Answer: Talk to a lawyer who specializes in such work. Tell the attorney exactly what happened to you, from the first time you visited your doctor through your last contact with him or her. What were the circumstances surrounding your illness or injury? How did your doctor treat it? What did your doctor tell you about your treatment? Did you follow your doctor's instructions? What happened to you? Answers to these and other relevant questions become important if you think your doctor may have committed malpractice. Like other personal injury claims, the case will either be settled or go to trial, usually before a jury [and, see, Chapter 2: Medical Malpractice, infra].

7. *Question: A disclaimer that came with the lawn mower said the manufacturer did not warrant it in any way. Will that defeat my claim?*

Answer: That is a product liability issue. While limited warranties are sometimes enforced by courts, full disclaimers often are not. Courts find such warranties invalid because you, as the consumer, are not in an equal bargaining position. They also rule that such clauses are unconscionable (grossly unfair) and contrary to public policy. Most courts limit the effect of limited warranties to repairs. A limited warranty is not a waiver of liability for injuries.[1]

Workers' Compensation 101

After many years in the business, an alligator wrestler decided to retire. Since he had paid his dues with many injuries on the job, he decided he should collect on his well-deserved benefits from his workers' compensation insurance.

He had an artificial right leg, a hook where his left hand used to be, and an artificial left eye. He was assured by his workers' compensation attorney that he would qualify for compensation if his injuries were work related.

"How did you get that artificial right leg?", the attorney asked.

"I was hunting alligators in the Louisiana swamp when my boat ran ashore, causing me to fall in the water, and a large alligator snapped my right leg off", the alligator wrestler answered.

"Work related for sure," the attorney commented. 'What about your left hand? How did you get the left hook?"

"Similar story," the man replied. "I was in my boat hunting for alligators in the swamp when a storm came up and rolled the boat. I fell out of the boat and a large alligator bit my left hand off."

---

[1]   [Excerpts in this chapter are taken and updated from the article, "Personal Injury 101: Questions & Answers," The Maryland Business Monthly, June 1998, by Charles Jerome Ware.]

"OK. That's work related too. Finally, how did you lose the left eye?" the attorney asked.

The alligator wrestler answered, "I was lying outside on my hammock at my boat house near the swamp when a bird flew over and unloaded itself into my left eye".

"So, what does that have to do with the loss of your left eye?" the attorney asked.

"I used my new left hook to clear my left eye!"

Workers' compensation, popularly referred to as "workers' comp", is a form of insurance designed to provide medical benefits and reimbursement for lost wages for covered employees who are injured on the job. In exchange and consideration for these benefits, the employee waives his or her rights to sue the employer for the tort of negligence. This tradeoff is often called the "compensation bargain."

Typically, workers' compensation will pay the employee's hospital and medical expenses that are necessary to diagnose and treat the on-the-job injury. Further, it can provide disability payments while the employee is unable to work (usually, about two-thirds of the employee's regular salary), and it may pay for the employee's rehabilitation, retraining, and some other benefits.

It should be noted that, although workers' compensation covers most on-the-job injuries, it does not cover all of them. There are limits to coverage. For instance, the following circumstances may not be covered by workers' compensation:

If the injuries occurred because—

(1) the employee was intoxicated or using illegal drugs at the time;
(2) the injuries were self-inflicted;
(3) the employee was committing a serious crime;
(4) the employee was not on the job;
(5) the employee's conduct violated company procedures or policy.

Worker's compensation not only covers injuries on the job, it also covers long-term on-the-job health problems and illnesses. It is not infrequent for workers to receive compensation for injuries and illnesses that are caused by misuse or overuse of the body over a substantial period of time. Some examples of this include:

(1) repetitive stress injuries such as carpal tunnel syndrome and chronic back pain problems; and

(2) diseases and illnesses that are the gradual result of work conditions, such as heart conditions, lung disease, stress-related digestive problems (e.g., ulcers, etc.).

In the workers' compensation meaning, "on-the-job" refers to "job-related" injuries. For instance, the employee's "on-the-job" or "job-related" injury could occur while the employee is out of the office or building, traveling on work business, doing a work-related errand, attending a work-related seminar, convention, symposium, or other function; and even attending a work-required social function (such as an office Christmas party, etc.).

Finally, it must be noted that not all employees are covered by workers' compensation, because not all employers are required to have workers' compensation insurance coverage. State laws vary on this requirement, which ordinarily depends on the number of employees, type of business, and type of work the employee is doing. Further, every state excludes certain types of workers. These exclusions vary from state to state but may include, for example, farm workers, domestic employees, and migrant workers (seasonal or casual workers).

<u>Summary</u>: Chapter One-Personal Injury 101.

1. Be aware and be patient. Too many consumers who are victims of personal injury settle their cases too soon; without full and proper medical treatment and physical rehabilitation.

2. Every personal injury claim or lawsuit has to be filed within a certain time period or time limit, called a "statute of limitations"

period. Each and every state has a "statute of limitations" period for various offenses.

3. Generally, an employee cannot receive workers' compensation insurance benefits as well as sue the employer for negligence concerning the same injury. This waiver of the employee's right to sue for negligence is called the "compensation bargain".

4. A limited warranty is not a waiver of product liability to the consumer.

Chapter Two

Medical Malpractice

What are some signs that a patient's health care provider may not be the best choice for them?:

— Your cardiologist walks into the exam room and, without proper tests or other inquiry, tells the patient that he or she needs a heart transplant.
— Your nurse in the hospital drops your thermometer on the floor, then picks it up and sticks it in your mouth without cleaning or sterilizing it.
— Your surgeon leaves utensils (instruments, sponges, etc.) in your body after performing surgery on you.
— Your dentist pulls the wrong tooth.
— Your psychiatrist advises you that suicide is indeed an option for you.
— Your marriage psychologist is dating your spouse.
— Neither the phlebotomist (blood collector), your nurse, nor your doctor can find your veins to draw blood.
— The urologist who has agreed to perform your vasectomy (surgery in the penis area to induce permanent sterility) has a severe case of the shakes.
— Your therapist to help you stop smoking recommends you switch from cigarettes to cigars.
— Your plastic surgeon clearly needs plastic surgery.
— Your hospital sits next to a mortuary, and a cemetery.
— Your alcohol counselor has a liquor bar in his or her office.

— Your diabetes doctor enters the exam room with a doughnut in one hand and a cola in the other.
— Your weight doctor is morbidly obese.

On a more serious note:

The healthcare system in the United States is arguably the best in the world. Not surprisingly, however, it is not perfect. Nothing is. Mistakes occur every day in every profession. Here are a few of the many questions, and their answers, concerning the complex subject of medical malpractice, providing a kind of "primer" on this subject for the layman:

1. *Question: What is medical malpractice?*

Answer: Medical malpractice is legally-recognized negligence committed by a professional healthcare provider—a doctor, nurse, dentist, technical, or hospital worker—whose performance of duties departs from a standard of practice of those with similar training and experience, resulting in legally-recognized harm to a patient or patients.

Most medical malpractice actions are filed against doctors who have failed to use "reasonable care" to treat patients. The medical profession itself sets the standard for malpractice by its own custom and practice. Historically, under the so-called "locality rule," a doctor was required only to possess and apply the knowledge and use the skill and care that was ordinarily used by reasonably well-qualified physicians in the locality, or similar locations, in which he or she practiced. But today the trend is toward abolishing such a rule in favor of a national standard of practice administered by the AMA (American Medical Association) or some other established medical institution.

Just about all medical malpractice cases mandate or require credible expert testimony. The primary reason for this requirement is that the medical facts in these cases are usually too complex for the average non-medical person to determine or make the decision whether the doctor or other medical professional should be held liable for the patient's injury.

In many states the complainant is required to get a medical expert's opinion before even starting a lawsuit.

No matter how egregious or awful the facts may seem in a potential medical malpractice case, credible expert medical testimony is usually necessary to make the case.

[see, inter alia, "The Four Elements of Medical Malpractice", Yale New Haven (Connecticut) Medical Center: Issues in Risk Management, info.med.yale.edu (1997); "Changing the Malpractice System", by Clive E. Reinhardt, The New York Times, October 1, 2010].

It should be remembered that not every unsuccessful or unfortunate medical conclusion is the result of medical malpractice. It depends on the specific facts of each case. Generally, there are no guarantees of medical results.

2. *Question: Over the past couple of decades or so hasn't there been continuous discussion about changing the way medical malpractice cases are handled?*

Answer: Yes. Throughout the 1980s and 1990s, and now into the 2000s, doctors and insurance industry members have said that there is a "malpractice crisis," with spiraling insurance premiums and unreasonably high jury verdicts. In response, several states (including Maryland) have passed laws capping damage awards, limiting attorney's fees and shortening the time period in which plaintiffs could bring malpractice suits (three years in Maryland). Some states have instituted no-fault liability for malpractice claims, and others, like Maryland, have developed arbitration panels to hear medical malpractice claims before they could be filed in court to be determined by a judge or jury.

Other "tort reforms" are frequently discussed, especially in election years, including reducing recovery for "pain and suffering" in malpractice lawsuits and reducing damages to take into account payments from insurance and workers' compensation.

3. *Question: How do I find out if I have a medical malpractice case?*

Answer: Talk to an attorney who specializes in this area of law. Describe to him or her exactly what happened to you, from the first time you visited your doctor through your last contact. Who" What? When? Where? How? etc. What were the circumstances surrounding your illness or injury? Who treated you? How were you treated for it? What did your doctor tell you about your treatment? When did all of this occur? Did you follow your doctor's instructions? What happened to you? Your answers to those and other relevant questions become critically important if you believe your doctor may have committed medical malpractice against you.

It is pretty much established in American law that a complainant or plaintiff must prove the following four (4) elements of the tort (civil wrong) of negligence for success in a medical malpractice case:

1. There must be a duty of care owed to the complainant/ plaintiff by the negligent health care provider or health care professional;
2. That duty of care (1, above) must be breached or broken by the health care provider or health care professional;
3. This breach caused the injury to the complainant/plaintiff; and
4. The complainant/plaintiff suffered damages as a result of this breach.

[see, "The Four Elements of Medical Malpractice", <u>Yale New Haven (Connecticut) Medical Center: Issues in Risk Management</u>, 1997; info.med.yale.edu].

Only about one in 5 medical malpractice claims against doctors results in monetary payout or some other settlement to the claimant. This is the case even though about one in 14 doctors has a malpractice claim filed against them each year [jobs.aol.com/articles/2011/08/18].

Remember: In general, there are no guarantees of medical results. In order to have a medical malpractice case, you must show an injury or damages that resulted from your doctor's deviation from the appropriate standard of care for your medical condition.

4. *Question: How does a jury (in most cases) or a judge (in some cases) decide whether a doctor's actions "were within the standards of good medical practice" or "departed from a standard of practice of those with similar training and experience," resulting in legally-recognized harm to a patient or patients?*

Answer: Experts. A jury or a judge will consider testimony by experts—usually other doctors—who will testify whether they believe your physician's actions followed standard medical practice or fell below the accepted standard of care. In deciding whether your heart surgeon or pulmonologist, for example, was negligent, a jury will be told to rely on expert testimony to determine what a competent heart surgeon or pulmonologist would have done under the same or similar circumstances. A specialist, a heart surgeon or pulmonologist, for example, is held to a higher standard of care than would be expected of a non-specialist.[2] Further, if the negligence is extremely obvious (e.g., obvious errors or omissions) the breach of the standard of care may, on rare occasions, be proven by the "doctrine of res ipsa loquistor": *the thing speaks for itself* [see, Issues in Risk Management, info.med.yale.edu (1997); Black's Law Dictionary; Barron's Law Dictionary].

---

[2]   [Excerpts in this chapter are taken and updated from the article, "Medical Malpractice: Questions & Answers," The Maryland Business Monthly, June 1997, by Charles Jerome Ware.]

5. *Question: Is there a limited time or time limit in which a medical malpractice case can be filed?*

Answer: Yes. There is a limited time in which a medical malpractice claim can be filed. This time limit varies from state to state, generally, and/or from jurisdiction to jurisdiction. These time limits are typically called "statutes of limitations", and ordinarily range from about two to five years depending upon the jurisdiction and type of case [The reader is strongly advised to consult with an attorney within his or her jurisdiction for more specific information].

Statute of limitation periods begin when a cause of action is deemed to have arisen or when a plaintiff had reason to know of the harm. Some reasons for status of limitation are that evidence can be diluted, corrupted, compromised, or even just disappear over time; and memories fade, scenes change, and companies (as well as individuals) can dispose of relevant records over time; making justice difficult to obtain.

<u>Summary</u>: Chapter Two—Medical Malpractice 101.

1. No matter how egregious or awful the facts may seem in a potential medical malpractice case, credible expert medical testimony is necessary to make the case.
2. In general, there are no guarantees of medical results.
3. The time limit or statute of limitations to file a claim for medical malpractice begins when the actual harm occurred or when the claimant (person injured) had reason to know of the harm.
4. Despite its problems, the healthcare system in the United States is still arguably the best in the world.

PART II
PERSONAL FINANCE

Chapter Three

Credit Bureaus, Credit Scores
and the Credit Business

Credit is big business. Very big business. In fact, the collection of your personal credit data, the processing and storage of this personal credit information, and the selling of your personal credit information is a multi-billion dollar business annually.

Credit collection is legalized invasion of privacy.

Quite frankly, the cost of money (or buying power) is greater now probably than at just about anytime in history. As a result, our society depends more upon credit than probably any other society in history. The entire mechanism or process of consumer credit, credit bureaus, credit scores and the business of credit is designed for immediate gratification of consumer demand for things and services.

Credit Bureaus and Credit Files

Bear in mind that credit bureaus generally are not government agencies.

Typically credit bureaus are private, profit-making companies that collect and sell your personal credit information or credit history. They make huge profits selling your credit histories and files to banks, mortgage lenders, credit card companies, department stores and other retail outlets, credit unions, insurance companies, employers, landlords, and many others. These customers and clients of the credit bureaus, in turn, use your personal credit information for various purposes, including assessment of your creditworthiness, to supplement applications for insurance, housing, employment, personal traits (for marriage and other relational purposes), among others.

Since their business is to sell personal information of yours, and make a lot of money doing so, credit bureaus are constantly searching for more of your personal information to sell. Without your personal information to sell, credit bureaus do not exist. [Turner, Michael A. et al., "Give Credit Where Credit Is Due", Political and Economic Research Council, 1].

The Big "3"

There are currently three (3) major credit bureaus: Equifax, Experian and TransUnion. Together the big "3" have thousands of branch locations throughout the United States. Each of these three behemoths maintains a personal file on virtually every identified adult in the United States. We are talking about millions of files.

Credit bureaus dig up most of their personal information on you from your creditors, such as credit card companies, mortgage lenders, department stores and other retailers, banks and credit unions, and other lenders. They also scour court records and other adjudicatory entities, searching for lawsuits against you, judgments and bankruptcy filings. Further, they screen carefully city and county record office files, state office files, and other locations to find, among other personal information, recorded taxes, judgments, mechanic's and other liens, as well as other claims against you [see, "Fact Sheet 6: How Private Is My Credit Report?" Privacy Rights Clearing House (PRC), September 2010, www.privacy-rights.org].

The Credit Report

In creating your personal credit report to sell to someone, a credit bureau usually searches its computer files until it find entries that match your name, Social Security number, address, and any other available identifying information. All matches are collected and constitute a credit report or credit file.

Information gathered on your credit report usually includes, among other things (1) your name, your aliases (if any), and any former names such as maiden names, etc.; (ii) past and present addresses; (iii) Social Security Number; (iv) employment history; (v) marriages; (vi) divorces; (vii) lawsuits; (viii) judgments against you; (ix) liens or legal claims on your property; (x) inquiries concerning your credit, and of course, (xi) bankruptcies. It should be noted that lawsuits you are involved in as a party may be on your report even if you did not lose the case. [Trudeau, Kevin, Debt Cures", Chapter 9, Equity Press (2008)].

Credit reports are frequently wrong. And, they are biased against you (see, "Inside FICO," *infra*). ["Mistakes Do happen: A look at Errors in Consumer Credit Reports", United States Public Interest Research Group (2006-06-15)].

Allegedly, the majority of information in your credit report or file is your "credit history," including both positive and negative data. The truth or reality of the matter, though, is that a major bias exists on the part of credit bureaus against the inclusion of positive or good credit information in you file; and a clear affinity or propensity by the credit reporting agencies is to seek, find, and report what negative data they can get on you.

In my many years of experience, I have yet to see a credit report or file that, for example, truly reflects a positive payment history; including early payments or pay-offs to the creditor.

Typically, your credit report or file contains (a) the name of "some" of your creditors, particularly the ones of which you may have been "untimely" in at least one payment; (b) the type and number of each of those questionable accounts; (c) when each of these accounts was opened; (d) the alleged "payment history" for the previous 24 to 36 months or so (usually whether you pay "on time" [not early] or, more importantly, to creditors and credit bureaus 30, 60, 90 or 120 days past due payments); (e) your credit limit or the original amount of the loan and your alleged credit balance; (f) information as to whether any accounts have been turned over to a collection agency; and (g) what inquiries have been made concerning your credit by third-parties such as potential creditors.

Occasionally, though not as frequently as they should, credit bureaus may report whether you are disputing a charge.

The Credit Score

First of all, the alleged one "credit score" for each person is a myth. There can be several "credit scores" for each individual. It depends simply upon the <u>source</u> of the "credit score." The higher the score, the better for the consumer.

As a consumer, you really are nothing but a number. The so-called "credit score" is allegedly calculated using a so-called "algorithm", an intimidating word meaning a complex mathematical formula. Diverse information about the consumer is placed into a computer and, using the algorithm selected by the credit reporting agency, a "credit score" is produced. The resulting score is usually between 300 and 850, for some reason. They could use numbers between 1 and 10, or between 1,000 and 10,000. I am convinced that ultimately the goal of the credit reporting agencies is to confuse and bedazzle the consumer.

In any event, this number—the "credit score"—is used by society for a variety of purposes: to determine interest rates you pay banks and other lenders such as credit card companies and mortgage companies, to get certain employment; to determine whether you "qualify" for a credit card, mortgage, or other loan; as well as other purposes.

The predominant so-called "credit score" software algorithm used in the United States is the one developed by a company named Fair Isaac Corporation or (FICO). Thus, the name "FICO" credit score. Fair Isaac is a Minneapolis-based financial services company.

This company, Fair Isaac, does <u>not</u> maintain a warehouse of data with various types and categories of information on the consumer. However, the three major credit reporting bureaus—Equifax, Experian and TransUnion—use the FICO software and do collect and warehouse this consumer data.

It gets worse. Allegedly, the FICO algorithm (complex mathematical formula) is "proprietary," and thus is treated as a secret. Like the formula for Coca-Cola, which is allegedly kept in a secret vault, or the recipe for Colonel Sanders Kentucky Fried Chicken.

To make matters even more confusing, even though the big "3" credit reporting agencies all use the FICO algorithm, your (the consumer's) credit score can, and usually does, vary depending upon which agency is reporting it and the kind or type of lender that requested your score. [Trudeau, Kevin, "Debt Cures", Chapter 10, Equity Press (2008)].

Ten (10) Tips and Secrets About Your Credit Score

1. Your FICO credit score cannot be lower than 300 nor higher than 850. It is, of course, a secret as to why this is so.
2. Oddly, history and track records show that, ideally, a score in the 800s is probably not any better for your credit position than a score in the 700s. In other words, it is probably worth it to improve your credit score (if possible) to the 600s and 700s, but beyond that range, it will probably not increase significantly your credit attractiveness to lenders. Again, it is an algorithmic secret as to why it is this way.
3. Though important, your credit score does not reflect your income, employment history or your assets. It also does not show whether you pay your rent or utilities on time. In other words, your credit report does not reflect your overall financial picture. It simply shows on a particular date in time a snapshot for the potential lender's or employer's individual interpretation as to your future credit success or failure. Unfortunate, but true.

4. Even if you pay off your credit card every month it does not necessarily increase your credit score or make you a lower credit risk. That is because credit reporting agencies are not aware whether you are paying your bill in full or carrying a balance forward on your credit cards each month. They only know the amount you owed on your most recent credit card statement.

   Secret/Tip: Since a crucial point is how much available credit you have used on your card, a key fact to remember is that it looks better when computing your credit score if you use less than half of your credit limit.

5. Taking advantage of "reward cards" or "reward programs" can and do affect your creditworthiness. It is believed that a large percentage of your FICO credit score is based on so-called "credit utilization." Credit utilization includes how much you have used of each credit limit, how much you have borrowed as a percentage of your total available credit, and how large your dollar balances are. This scenario can be credit hurtful for the "rewards" enthusiast.

   Secret/Tip: I recommend that the consumer keep his or her balances lower by cutting back on his or her credit use for two months or more before applying for a new mortgage or car loan, or other major purchase. This step will help improve your credit score, at least it appears to.

6. An apparently important factor in your credit score is whether you have made late payments; even though you may have since paid the debt in full. Late payments account for a sizeable percentage of your total credit score.

7. Bad information can frequently stay on your credit report for up to ten (10) years. Good credit information can remain on your report for about as long. For example, closed accounts in good standing can remain on your credit report for up to 10 years or more. In fact, some credit experts recommend that consumers

do not formally close a so-called good-standing account, but instead let the issuer close it for lack of activity. Presumably, the good credit history adds to your creditworthiness long-term. However, if the credit card company is charging you to keep the account open but unused, it is <u>not</u> worth it in my opinion.

8. Free credit score reports are worth about what you pay for them. They rarely, if ever, reflect or show the scores that lenders request and see about the consumer. Free credit score reports, and generally most credit score reports you pay for, are usually not your so-called "real" scores.

9. "Soft" credit score inquiries should not affect your FICO score. But, again, frequently they do. These inquiries are the ones in which (i) you check your score; (ii) when your current credit card company keeps track of your credit; or (iii) when someone or some lender allegedly "preapproves" the consumer for credit, among others.

10. "Hard" credit score inquiries can, and frequently do, adversely affect the consumer's FICO credit score. These inquiries are the ones in which (i) you apply for a loan or credit; (ii) you open a new bank account; and (iii) you make a major purpose, such as a car (even if you pay cash for the item) among others.

<u>Secret/Tip</u>: Ask straightforwardly at the beginning if a bank, insurance company, or automobile dealer, etc., plans to check your credit record. Multiple credit inquiries over at least a period of several weeks could hamper your credit score for a year or more. However, multiple inquiries over a very short period of time—say, a week or so—sometimes count as only one "hard" inquiry. [www.pueblo.gsa.gov/cic; Trudeau, Kevin, "Debt Cures", Equity Press (2008)].

<u>Inside FICO</u>

The FICO credit score (or Fair Isaac Corporation credit score) does not favor the average citizen. This complex mathematical algorithm software is said to essentially analyze the target consumer's habits over the last two years. Of course, we are not supposed to be sure of this because, remember, the FICO algorithm is "proprietary" and therefore "secret."

I am informed that your FICO score is principally concerned with your payment history and how much you owe. Only a few of FICO's rating factors are positive in nature, and most factors are negative! Most consumers never stand a chance with these odds against him or her. [Finance-commerce.com/2011; Trudeau, "Debt Cures", Equity Press (2008)].

Credit Cards

Credit card companies are among the most prolific users of FICO credit scores, and thus among the biggest and most lucrative customers of credit bureaus.

Increasingly, in many states such as Minnesota for example, delinquent credit card debt can be the underlying cause for consumers being jailed or imprisoned [see, Chapter 19, infra, "Avoiding Debtors' Prison In The United States"]. This is happening increasingly, for instance, when the consumer debtor misses a civil debt collection court hearing for an alleged unpaid debt. Frequently, it is a credit card debt.

Unlike many countries, in America it is not supposed to be a crime to owe money any more. And, debtors' prisons were abolished in the United States in the 19th century (specifically, in 1833). However, increasingly American citizens and others are routinely imprisoned in this country for failing to pay debts.

It is interesting to note that Minnesota, which is probably the most creditor-friendly state in the United States, is also the home base or headquarters for FICO (the Fair Isaac Corporation).

In general, credit cards probably should be treated as your enemy; not your friend. They are sometimes convenient in our lives, but not truly necessary for most people. Settle your credit card debt, and be cautious with your use of credit cards in the future. Enough said?

The Federal Trade Commission and Credit

The United States Federal Trade Commission, or FTC, is an independent agency of the United States government which was established in 1914 during President Woodrow Wilson's administration by the Federal Trade Commission Act. The FTC's stated principal mission is the promotion of "consumer protection" and the elimination and prevention of what regulators perceive to be harmfully "anticompetitive" business practices, such as coercive monopoly.

As former Special Counsel to the Chairman of the FTC, I recall vividly that the Agency or Commission has always considered itself to be the premier protector of the American consumer.

One of the many responsibilities of the Commission—which is headed by five commissioners, one of whom serves as the Chairman—is the protection of American consumer credit reporting rights. It is the Federal Trade Commission that administers the federal Fair Credit Reporting Act (FCRA). Among other things, the Fair Credit Reporting Act requires each of the nationwide consumer reporting companies—currently, Equifax, Experian and TransUnion—to provide the consumer with a free copy of his or her credit report, at the consumer's request, once every twelve (12) months. ["Report to Congress on the Fair Credit Reporting Act Dispute Process", Federal Trade Commission (FTC) and the Board of Governors of the Federal Reserve System (FRS), August 2006].

A Summary of Major Consumer Rights Under the Fair Credit Reporting Act (FCRA)

[www.ftc.gov/os/statutes; Text of the Fair Credit Reporting Act, 15 U.S.C. § 1681 (a); www.gao.gov1new.items]

1. It is important to note that the FCRA was enacted to promote the accuracy, fairness and privacy of consumer information in the files and databases of consumer reporting agencies.

2. There are many types of consumer reporting agencies: including credit bureaus, and specialty credit reporting agencies such as those firms that sell information about consumer check writing histories, medical records, rental history records, and so forth.

3. For more information, including information about additional rights, go to www.ftc.gov/credit or write to: Consumer Response Center, Room 130-A, Federal Trade Commission, 600 Pennsylvania Ave., N.W., Washington, D.C. 20580.

    Para information en español, visite www.ftc.gove/credit o escribe a la FTC Consumer Response Center, Room 130-A, 600 Pennsylvania Ave., N.W., Washington, D.C. 20580.

4. **The consumer must be informed if information in the credit file has been used against them.** Anyone who uses a credit report or another type of consumer report to deny your application for credit, insurance, or employment—or to take another adverse action against you—must tell you, and must give you the name, address, and phone number of the agency that provided the information.

5. **The consumer has the right to know what is in his or her credit file.** You may request and obtain all the information about you in the files of a consumer reporting agency (your "file disclosure"). You will be required to provide proper identification which may include your Social Security number. In many cases, the disclosure will be free. You are entitled to a free file disclosure if:

    (a) person or business has taken adverse action against you because of information in your credit report;

    (b) you are the victim of identity theft and place a fraud alert in your file;

    (c) your file contains inaccurate information as a result of fraud;

    (d) you are on public assistance;

    (e) you are unemployed but expect to apply for employment within 60 days.

In addition, as of September 2005, all consumers are entitled to one free disclosure every 12 months upon request from each nationwide credit bureau and from nationwide specialty consumer reporting agencies. Go to www.ftc.gov/credit for additional information.

6. The consumer has the right to request and receive his or her "credit score" from the credit reporting agency (or "credit bureau").

    As we have discussed previously in this chapter, supra ("The Credit Score" and "Tips and Secrets About Your Credit Score"), the consumer's credit score can, and frequently does, vary between the so-called "Big 3" credit bureaus of Equifax, Experian and TransUnion. Remember—and never forget—these credit scores are proprietary and make a lot of money for these giant companies.

    Generally, the consumer does not have just one credit score, but several scores. The consumer's FICO credit score, developed and owned by a billion-dollars in annual revenues company based in Minneapolis, Minnesota by the name of Fair Isaac Corporation (FICO™), can vary depending upon which credit bureau is reporting it.

    FICO credit scores are calculated using a secret, proprietary, complex mathematical formula called an "algorithm." Essentially, the scores are numerical summaries of the consumer's "credit-worthiness" based upon specific information received and evaluated about the consumer.

    It has been unofficially reported that—in all of its secret, proprietary, complex mathematical, algorithmic calculations—about six (6) FICO rating factors are "positive" and about 88 are "negative." In other words, the FICO algorithm is searching for 88 negative things that can be used in the calculation against the consumer. [Trudeau, "Debt Cures", Chapter 10, Equity Press (2008)].

7. The consumer may, and should, request a credit score from consumer reporting agencies that create these scores or distribute

the scores used in residential real property loans. **Though they may have to pay for the report, there is no harm in the consumer requesting a free copy.**

8. **The consumer has the right to dispute the incomplete or inaccurate information.** If the consumer identifies information in his or her file that they believe is incomplete or inaccurate, they should immediately report it to the consumer reporting agency. The agency <u>must</u> investigate the consumer's complaint or concern, unless the complaint or concern is completely frivolous.

   Some basic credit dispute procedures can be found at <u>www.ftc.gov/credit</u>, along with an explanation of them.

9. **Consumer reporting agencies must correct or delete inaccurate, incomplete, or unverifiable information found in the consumer's credit file.** Inaccurate, incomplete or unverifiable information <u>must</u> be removed or corrected from the consumer's file, usually within 30 days. The consumer reporting agency may, however, continue to report the consumer's information the agency has verified as accurate.

10. **Consumer reporting agencies may <u>not</u> report outdated or outmoded negative information.** In most cases, a consumer reporting agency may not report negative information that is more than seven years old, or bankruptcies that are more than 10 years old.

11. **Access to the consumer's credit file is limited, by law.** A consumer reporting agency may provide information about the consumer only to persons with valid, demonstrated need for the credit information. Usually, this "valid need" includes, for example, an application with a creditor, insurer, employer, landlord, or other business by the consumer. The FCRA actually specifies those persons with a valid need for access to the consumer's credit file.

12. **Consumer credit reports cannot be provided or given to the consumer's employers or potential employers without the consumer's prior written consent.** The one exception to required "written" consent that I can think of is the trucking

industry. For more information on this issue, reference is made to www.ftc.gov/credit.

13. **The consumer has the right and opportunity to limit so-called "prescreened" offers of credit and insurance he or she receives (usually in the mail or via the Internet) based allegedly on information in the consumer's credit report.** Unsolicited "prescreened" offers for credit and insurance must include a toll-free number you can call if you choose to remove your name and address from the lists these offers are based on. You may opt-out with the nationwide credit bureaus at 1-888-5-OPTOUT (1-888-567-8688).

14. **If harmed by violations of his or her credit rights, the consumer can sue for damages against the violator(s).** If a consumer reporting agency, or, in some cases, a user of consumer reports or a furnisher of information to a consumer reporting agency violates the FCRA, you may be able to sue in state or federal court.

15. **Consumer identity theft victims and active duty military have additional legal rights under the FCRA.** For more information, inquire on-line at www.ftc.gov/credit.
    For additional information on "identity theft," see Chapter Five, infra.

16. States may enforce the **Fair Credit Report Act (FCRA)**, and many states have their own consumer reporting laws. In some cases, you may have more rights under state law. For more information, contact your state or local consumer protection agency or your state Attorney General. Federal enforcement of the FCRA include, thus far, the following agencies:

TYPE OF BUSINESS:	CONTACT:
Consumer reporting agencies, creditors and others not listed below	Federal Trade Commission: Consumer Response Center—FCRA Washington, DC 20580　　　1-877-382-4357
National banks, federal branches/agencies of foreign banks (word "National" or initials "N.A." appear in or after bank's name)	Office of the Comptroller of the Currency Compliance Management, Mail Stop 6-6 Washington, DC 20219　　　800-613-6743
Federal Reserve System member banks (except national banks, and federal branches/agencies of foreign banks)	Federal Reserve Consumer Help (FRCH) P.O. Box 1200 Minneapolis, MN 55480 Telephone: 888-851-1920 Website Address: www.federalreserveconsumerhelp.gov Email Address: ConsumerHelp@FederalReserve.gov
Savings associates and federally chartered savings banks (word "Federal" or initials "F.S.B." appear in federal institution's name)	Office of Thrift Supervision Consumer Complaints Washington, DC 20552　　　800-842-6929
Federal credit unions (words "Federal Credit Union" appear in institution's name)	National Credit Union Administration 1775 Duke Street Alexandria, VA 22314　　　703-519-4600
State-chartered banks that are not members of the Federal Reserve System	Federal Deposit Insurance Corporation Consumer Response Center 2345 Grand Avenue, Suite 100 Kansas City, MO 64108-2638　　1-877-275-3342
Air, surface, or rail common carriers regulated by former Civil Aeronautics Board or Interstate Commerce Commission	Department of Transportation Office of Financial Management Washington, DC 20590　　　202-366-1306
Activities subject to the Packers and Stockyards Act, 1921	Department of Agriculture Office of Deputy Administrator—GIPSA Washington, DC 20250　　　202-720-7051

17. **Get your free annual credit report!** You can order your free annual credit report at annualcreditreport.com, by calling 1-877-322-8228, or by completing the Annual Credit Report Request Form and mailing it to: Annual Credit Report Request Service, P.O. Box 105281, Atlanta, GA 30348-5281. When you order, you need to provide your name, address, Social Security number, and date of birth. To verify your identity, you may need to provide some information that only you would know, like the amount of your monthly mortgage payment.

18. **Beware, and avoid, "Imposter" credit report websites**. The Federal Trade Commission (FTC) advises consumers who order their free annual credit report online to be sure to correctly spell annualcreditreport.com or link to it from the FTC's website to avoid being misdirected to other websites that offer supposedly free reports, but only with the purpose of selling other products. While consumers may be offered additional products or services while on the authorized website, they are not required to make a purchase to receive their free annual credit reports.

<u>SUMMARY</u>: Chapter Three—Credit Bureaus, Credit Scores and the Credit Business

1. Credit collection is a multi-billion dollar business annually; very big business.

2. Credit collection is legalized invasion of privacy. Credit agencies are always digging up personal information on consumers.

3. Currently, the "Big 3" major credit bureaus are Equifax, Experian, and TransUnion. They are private companies, <u>not</u> government agencies. They make lots of money.

4. Lawsuits the consumer is involved in may be on his or her credit report even if the consumer did not lose the case.

5. Credit reports are frequently wrong . . . to the consumer's detriment. The major interest of credit bureaus is to make money, not report your credit properly.

6. Credit reports, generally, are biased against the consumer. An affinity or propensity by the credit reporting agencies is

to seek, find, and report what negative data they can get on the consumer. They are <u>not</u> particularly concerned with the consumer's positive credit information.

7. The alleged one "credit score" for each consumer or person is a myth. Among the major credit reporting agencies there can be several different "credit scores" for each individual.

8. The predominant so-called "credit score" software algorithm (complex mathematical formula) used by the "Big 3" major credit reporting agencies in the United States—Equifax, Experian, and TransUnion—is called FICO, named after the company that developed it: Fair Isaac Corporation.

9. FICO was developed by a company headquartered in Minneapolis, Minnesota by the name of Fair Isaac Corporation (or FICO). It is a multi-billion financial services company with over 2,000 employees.

10. Your FICO score is inherently unfair since, among other reasons, it is proprietary (money-making) and thus is treated as a secret. Therefore, no consumer or individual has the capacity to compute his or her own FICO score.

11. Generally, your FICO credit score cannot be lower than 300 nor higher than 850. Again, it's a secret as to why.

12. Oddly, FICO history and track records show that, ideally, a credit score in the 800s is probably not any better for the consumer's credit position than a credit score in the 700s. In other words, a credit score higher than the 700s will probably not increase significantly the average consumer's credit attractiveness to lenders.

13. Your credit score does not reflect your overall financial picture. Though important in our society, your credit score does not reflect your income, employment history or your assets. It certainly reveals little about your character.

14. Even if you pay off your credit card every month it does not necessarily increase your credit score or make you a lower credit risk. Hmmm . . . go figure.

15. Since a crucial point in credit worthiness and credit reporting is how much available credit the consumer has used on his or

her card, it is important to remember that it looks better for the consumer when computing their FICO credit score if the consumer uses less than half of their credit limit.

16. Since it is believed that about 30% of the consumer's FICO credit score is based upon so-called "credit utilization," taking advantage of popular "reward cards" or "reward programs" can and do affect the consumer's creditworthiness . . . and can be hurtful credit-wise for the "rewards" enthusiast.

17. It is recommended that the consumer keep his or her balances lower by cutting back on his or her credit use for about two months or so before applying for major purchase loans such as a new mortgage or car loan. This step should help improve your credit score.

18. Late payments are believed to account for a sizeable amount of your total FICO credit score, even though you may have since paid the debt in full.

19. It is true that negative information will frequently stay on your FICO credit report for up to 7 years.

20. Positive credit information can remain on your FICO credit report for longer than seven years.

21. Generally, if you have positive credit information on your credit report, it is recommended that you leave it there. Presumably, the good credit history adds to your creditworthiness long-term.

22. Generally, free credit reports are worth about what you pay for them: nothing. These free reports rarely, if ever, reflect or show the so-called "real" scores that lenders request and see. Free credit reports tend to be more frightening than helpful.

23. "Soft" credit score inquiries should not affect you FICO credit score. These inquiries are the ones in which (i) you check on your score, (ii) your current lender checks your credit, (iii) some potential lender allegedly "pre-approves" you for credit, among others. By the way, there is no such thing as "pre-approval" for credit.

24. "Hard" credit score inquiries can, and frequently do, negatively affect your FICO credit score. These inquiries occur when (i) you apply for a loan or credit, (ii) you open a bank account, (iii)

you make a major purchase such as a home or car, among others. Everytime you request or ask for credit, you are punished by a "hard" credit score inquiry.

25. It is recommended that the consumer ask straight forwardly at the beginning if a bank, insurance company, or automobile dealer, etc., intends to check his or her credit record. Multiple "hard" credit inquiries over a period of several weeks could hamper the consumer's credit score for a year or more.

26. In general, credit cards should be treated as your <u>enemy</u>; not your friend. They can be convenient in our lives, but they are not truly necessary for most consumers.

27. The United States Federal Trade Commission (or FTC) considers itself to be the premier protector of the American consumer; and, in particular, American consumer credit reporting rights. It is the FTC that administers the federal Fair Credit Report Act (FCRA), to promote accuracy, fairness, and privacy of consumer credit information.

28. Among other requirements, the Fair Credit Reporting Act (FCRA) mandates each of the nationwide consumer reporting companies—currently Equifax, Experian and TransUnion—to provide the consumer with a free copy of his or her credit report, at the consumer's request, once every (12) months.

29. For more information on consumer credit report rights, visit the following website: <u>www.ftc.gov/credit</u>; or write:

> Consumer Response Center
> Federal Trade Commission
> Room 130-A
> 600 Pennsylvania Avenue, N.W.
> Washington, D.C. 20580

30. The law requires that the consumer must be informed if information in the credit file has been used against them.

31. The law gives the consumer the right to know what is in his or her credit file.

32. The law gives the consumer the right to request and receive his or her "credit score" from each credit reporting agency.

33. The law gives the consumer the right to dispute any and all incomplete and inaccurate information in their credit file or report.

34. The law requires that consumer reporting agencies correct or delete inaccurate, incomplete, or unverifiable information found in the consumers' credit file, usually within 30 days of notice of this information.

35. The law requires that consumer reporting agencies not report "outdated" or "outmoded" negative information.

36. By law, access to the consumer's credit file is limited. In other words, not everyone is allowed access to your personal credit information.

37. By law, consumer credit reports cannot be given to the consumer's employers or potential employers without the consumer's prior written consent.

38. The law permits consumers to sue for damages against violators if harmed by violations of his or her credit rights.

39. If you are active duty military or a consumer identity theft victim, the law grants you additional rights under the Fair Credit Reporting Act (FCRA). See, www.ftc.gov/credit.

Chapter Four

Fifteen (15) Tips for Avoiding Foreclosure

"Produce the note!"

Whenever clients and other homeowners, and even commercial building owners call me concerning possible foreclosure proceedings against them, I almost always advise them to request that the foreclosing party, or plaintiff, **"produce the note"** on the property.

It is no less than remarkable how many times your promissory note on the property can be misfiled, made unavailable temporarily, or even lost between the transfer of your note from one creditor (mortgagor) to another. It is the mortgagee's right to have the note produced by the mortgagor prior to final foreclosure. This factor frequently buys valuable time for the mortgagee (borrower).

Some experts have predicted or assessed that upwards of forty percent of mortgage notes cannot be produced by the mortgagor or lender upon demand [www.proofofnote.com].

The major GOALS of the "produce the note" or "produce the document" strategy are:

1. To make certain the alleged mortgagor or institution suing the homeowner in foreclosure is, in fact, the owner of the mortgage note. The bottom line is that there is only one original note for each mortgage that has the homeowner's signature on it. It is this document, the "note" that proves the homeowner owes the mortgage debt.

2. To fend off and fight sleazy, unscrupulous and possibly fraudulent foreclosure procedures being used by banks, credit unions and other mortgagors to dupe homeowners during foreclosures.
3. To maintain and/or encourage fundamental "due process" in foreclosure proceedings, so that homeowners cannot be deprived of their property without constitutionally-mandated safeguards.

[commonlaw.findlaw.com/2009/02/produce-the-note-foreclosure-delay-tactic; www.consumerwarmingnetwork.com/2008/06/19/produce-the-note; www.proofofnote.com].

Nationwide, courts generally have responded favorably to the "produce the note" strategy. After all, lawyers and judges are trained to expect, want, and appreciate the legal and constitutional concept of "due process" that producing the note argues for.

Most courts will delay foreclosure proceedings until the courts are satisfied that the lender has engaged in due diligence and good-faith efforts to locate and present the original mortgage note. Some courts, however, have gone so far as to find that a lender or mortgagor cannot complete or perfect a foreclosure if they cannot produce the original note.

STRATEGY

The strategy is not to help the consumer get his house for free. The real strategy is to delay the foreclosure procedures so as to pressure the mortgagor or lender to negotiate or to buy time for the consumer to explore other options besides foreclosure.

FORECLOSURE

Without a doubt, losing one's home or commercial business building through foreclosure, i.e., forced sale of the property in order to pay back the loan, is an unmitigated nightmare.

Generally, the home is the subject of foreclosure, and it takes place when a homeowner cannot repay his or her loan according to the terms of the mortgage agreement with the lender (mortgagor). When this occurs, the mortgagor (lender) may start [foreclosure] legal proceedings to have the mortgagee's (borrower's) home or property sold (usually auctioned). Then the proceeds from the sale or auction of the property are used to help pay off the outstanding debt on the property.

In these turbulent economic and financial times, foreclosures are unfortunately all too prevalent in our communities. This is the case despite the fact that most lenders historically try to avoid foreclosure because the process is costly, takes a long time, and does not guarantee full and complete recovery of the loan amount. Foreclosure laws vary from state to state, but foreclosure proceedings generally follow a consistent series of steps, which are summarized as follows:

1. The Promissory Note and/or Mortgage. Remember, *supra*, **"produce the note!"** When the consumer took out his or her home or commercial business loan, they usually had to sign a promissory note and a mortgage. Both documents usually contain clauses that set forth the consumer's rights and responsibilities regarding repayment of the loan as well as the lender's (mortgagor's) rights and responsibilities.

2. First Missed Payment by the Consumer. Usually, when the consumer misses a payment, the lender is routinely required to send the consumer a letter of reminder, which is usually accompanied with an imposed lawful and agreed-upon late fee.

3. Letter of Notice of Default. If the consumer still fails to pay, the lender is required to send the consumer a formal "Notice of Default" before taking any further action against the consumer. This "Notice" should inform the consumer that he or she can "cure" the default within a specified period of time by making the payments as well as pay any additional fees that have accrued. The "Notice of Default" should specifically state the exact amount the consumer owes as well as the deadline in which it must be paid.

It is important to note that the lender is obligated to send this notice to your last known address; but the consumer is required to diligently inform the lender of his or her current address.

4. <u>Mitigation</u>. If the consumer pays the full amount owed within the specified time limit, and then continues timely payments, the lender is prohibited from taking further action against the consumer. **If the consumer cannot make the mortgage payments in a timely manner, he or she can still avoid foreclosure by selling the home themselves.**

5. <u>"The Deed in lieu of Foreclosure" or "Short Sale"</u>.

Many homeowners facing foreclosure decide that they simply cannot afford to stay in their home. After all, no homeowner who has a mortgage is ever fully and totally immune or safe from the possibility of foreclosure. Financial setbacks such as a major illness, physical and/or mental disability, or loss of income (employment, etc.) can and frequently do affect most people. Two options for the homeowner who decides to give up their home but want to avoid foreclosure and its negative impact on the consumer's credit are to consider (i) the "deed in lieu of foreclosure" or the "short sale" [<u>see</u>, "Short Sales and Deeds in Lieu of Foreclosure", www.nolo.com/legal-encyclopedia/short-sales-deeds-lieu-foreclosure].

<u>The Short Sale</u>. The homeowner who has encountered and can demonstrate genuine financial hardship may be eligible for a "short sale" of their home, in which the lender (mortgagor) agrees to take a loss on the mortgage loan in order for the homeowner to sell the house before foreclosure proceedings occur. The short sale requires the lender's (mortgagor's) cooperation. Many states allow lenders (mortgagors) to sue the homeowner for the remaining deficiency even after the house is foreclosed upon or sold. In these states it is crucial that the homeowner gets the lender's agreement <u>in writing</u> not to sue him or her for the "deficiency".

The "deficiency" occurs when the amount the homeowner owes on the home mortgage loan is <u>more</u> than the proceeds from the sale or auction of the house. In other words, the sale price of the house falls "short" of the amount the homeowner owes the lender [<u>see</u>, www.nolo.com, <u>supra</u>; and, www.lendingtree.com/smartborrower/ home-loan-help/manging-your-mortgage]. Said another way, the difference between the loan balance and the sale price of the house is the amount of the "deficiency".

Beware of Tax Consequences with the "Short Sale".

> The consumer should be aware that the "short sale" could, and usually does, generate tax consequences. The homeowner's "deficiency" amount may be charged to the consumer homeowner as taxable income (1099, etc.) under Internal Revenue Service (IRS) rules, procedures, and regulations. Generally, the IRS treats the "deficiency" as forgiven debt and thus taxable income subject to regular income tax [<u>see</u>, Nolo and <u>Learning Tree</u>, <u>supra</u>; and consult a tax attorney and/or accountant]. There are some exceptions for tax years 2007, 2008, and 2009 [<u>Ibid</u>.].

Very similar to "deeds in lieu of foreclosure", mortgagors (or lenders) are required to file 1099C statements with the Internal Revenue Service (IRS) when the "forgiven" (cancelled) debt is over $600 [www.bills.com].

<u>The Deed in Lieu of Foreclosure</u>. The "deed in lieu of foreclosure" transfers the house to the lender in a process that is faster, simpler and less costly than foreclosure [<u>see</u>, "Short Sale vs. Deed in Lieu", www.lendingtree.com/smartborrower; "Short Sales and Deeds in Lieu of Foreclosure", www.nolo.com/legal]. With the "deed in lieu of foreclosure" the homeowner transfers the house over to the lender/mortgagor—transfers the deed—in exchange for cancellation of the loan balance by the lender. In exchange, the lender promises to not initiate foreclosure proceedings against the homeowner, and/or to terminate any existing foreclosure proceedings against

the homeowner. Again, as with the "short sale", the homeowner is cautioned and/or warned to get this agreement or understanding with the lender/mortgagor <u>in writing</u>; particularly the agreement that the lender <u>forgives</u> any "deficiency" (the amount of the loan that is not covered by the sale proceeds) that remains after the house is sold [<u>see</u>, ezinearticles.com/short sale or Deed in Lieu of Foreclosure].

Beware of Tax Consequences with the "deed in lieu of Foreclosure".

Similar to the "short sale", <u>supra</u>, a deed in lieu of foreclosure may produce unfortunate taxable income (1099, etc.) based on the amount of the consumers/homeowner's forgiven debt [<u>ibid.</u>]. The homeowner and more generally—all consumers, should understand that "forgiven debt" (i.e., cancelled debt) by a creditor frequently means "taxable income" to the consumer.

As with most things in life, neither the "short-sale" nor the "deed-in-lieu of foreclosure" will guarantee that the consumer's credit will be undiminished. However, neither is as detrimental as foreclosure. In many cases, though, the tax consequences may be mitigated if the debt is eliminated in <u>bankruptcy</u> or the homeowner is declared <u>insolvent</u> [www.lendingtree.com/smartborrower/home-loan-help].

6. **The Foreclosure Lawsuit.** Foreclosure filings, frequently referred to as default notices, increased by almost 19% from 2008 to 2009 in the United States. In October 2009, 1 in 385 households in the United States had received a foreclosure notice. [CNBC.com/id/29655038]

    (i)   If the consumer does not pay the amount owed by the date due, **and cannot or does not sell the home themselves**, the lender may initiate foreclosure proceedings by suing the consumer for the unpaid balance of the loan. Keep in mind, the consumer also has the option of renting his or her home.

(ii)   In doing so, (i) *supra*, the lender will be asking the court to foreclose on the mortgage; that is, to bar the consumer from redeeming the mortgage or paying it off—and asking the court to order that the property be sold, or auctioned. **The proper court must be selected by the lender to file these proceedings**.

(iii)   The consumer must be named as a defendant (or respondent) in the foreclosure lawsuit, along with third parties who may have an interest in the property (such as other creditors who may want the property sold to repay them, or government agencies that may have claims for unpaid taxes).

(iv)   These third parties (usually the IRS, et al.) must have legitimate and proper "liens" on the consumer's property.

(v)   The foreclosure complaint or petition must be "served upon" (delivered to) the consumer by lawful and proper means as specified by the court's procedure and law; which usually means by the sheriff or by certified mail, etc.

(vi)   It is very important that, upon receipt of the foreclosure complaint or petition, the consumer or defendant/respondent contact an attorney immediately; regardless as to whether the consumer believes or feels he or she was properly served or not.

(vii)   Time is of the essence. A qualified attorney may be able to have the foreclosure lawsuit stopped for a number of possible reasons.

(viii)   Given enough time and effort, the attorney may be able to come to some agreement with the lender/mortgagor on behalf of the consumer.

(ix)   Finally, a qualified attorney can advise the consumer whether he or she should seek bankruptcy protection, which ordinarily and at least temporarily stops foreclosure proceedings. This legal maneuver is particularly helpful when the consumer is having difficulty paying his or her other bills.

(x)   Additionally, it should be noted that if the consumer is in default by at least three (3) payments, and their mortgage is insured by the Federal Housing Administration (FHA), the consumer may be able to avoid foreclosure by means of the mortgage Assignment Program administered by the Department of Housing and Urban Development (HUD).

(xi)   Obtain more mortgage company, appropriate government websites, and respected mortgage-involved specific information about this program and/or mortgage modification programs from related organizations.

(xii)   If the lender (mortgagor) proves its case against the consumer (mortgagee)—i.e., the lender has satisfied its obligations but the borrower (consumer) has defaulted on the mortgage—the court will grant a judgment for the mortgagor and against the mortgagee. This opens the door for the property to be sold.

(xiii) Sheriff's Sale or Judicial Sale. The court ordered sale of the property is known as a judicial sale or sheriff's sale, and it is usually carried out by a so-called "public auction" which is usually held at the local courthouse.

"Notice" to the public of a judicial sale is ordinarily governed by state law, and usually occurs by publication in the local newspaper.

(xiv)   Another Chance. After the "notice" is published locally, and prior to the actual sale or auction of the property, many lenders will give the consumer another chance to make good on the mortgage loan by paying the amount due and owing, plus penalties, interest, attorney fees and costs.

(xv)   Deficiency Judgment. If the homeowner still cannot pay the lender, the property will be sold to the highest bidder. When this happens, the consumer must move out of the house, often immediately. If the property is sold for less than the total amount owed on it (owed on the mortgage loan), a deficiency judgment could be pursued against the consumer by the lender.

(xvi) <u>Court Auditor's Report</u>. Further, in addition to the "deficiency judgment," (xv) *supra,* the Court Auditor, in his or her Report, could find additional monetary deficiencies that the lender and/or trustee may levy against the consumer.

(xvii) <u>Redemption After Foreclosure</u>. Owning one's home has historically been a sentimentally important factor in American life. Therefore, in an effort to provide the homeowning-consumer the maximum possible opportunity to keep his or her home, many states allow a "period of redemption after foreclosure" and sale in which the consumer can redeem their home and buy it back.

During this period of time after foreclosure and sale, the consumer sometimes can stay in the house. If the consumer pays the entire amount owed to the lender within the statutory "redemption" period, including all foreclosure fees and costs, they have now "redeemed" the property. The person who bought the property at the foreclosure sale must, of course, be refunded their money.

(xviii) <u>"Right of Redemption"</u>. To better understand "right of redemption" laws, it may be useful to better understand that there are generally two (2) types of foreclosures: (1) judicial foreclosures and (2) non-judicial foreclosures. As to whether the consumer has a "right of redemption" depends upon the state in which the property is located. Some states do not allow redemption [<u>see</u>, <u>www.bills. com/right-of-redemption-foreclosure</u>].

Generally, the concept of "right of redemption" is the ability or capacity of the former homeowner or property owner of a foreclosed property to redeem or reclaim the property after the foreclosure [<u>Ibid</u>.]. In characteristic and marginally understandable legalese, it means the right "to purchase back; to regain possession by payment of a stipulated price; repurchase [139 N.W. 802, 803]; the process of canceling and annulling a defeasible title, such as is created by a mortgage or tax sale, by paying the debt or fulfilling other conditions [255 P. 2d 957, 960]." See <u>Barron's</u> and <u>Black's</u> law dictionaries at "redemption", <u>interalia</u>.

(xix) <u>Time Limit to Redeem Property After Foreclosure</u>: For those states that allow redemption after foreclosure, the time limit for redeeming real estate after a foreclosure sale may depend on the size and type of property and the amount of debt involved. **With regard to any particular or specific state or jurisdiction, the reader and/or the consumer is urged to seek qualified attorney assistance with any questions regarding the topic of redemption after foreclosure** [also see, www.foreclosurefish.com/blog; law.onecle. com; www.foreclosedreams.com/right-of-redemption; en.allexperts.com/realestatehomemortage; realestate. findlaw.com].

With the warning and the urging that the reader and consumer seek advice and counsel from qualified attorneys and others with specific questions and inquiries concerning any and all subjects, topics and issues in this book, it is observed generally that:

— There is no right of redemption after sale in foreclosure in the jurisdictions of Maryland, Delaware, Pennsylvania, New York, West Virginia, Ohio, District of Columbia, Connecticut, North Carolina, South Carolina, Georgia, Florida, Indiana, Mississippi, Louisiana, Oklahoma, Texas and Hawaii [www.ehow.com/info; <u>www.google. com/U.S.Foreclosurelaws</u>];

— The redemption period is set by the appropriate court in Virginia;

— The redemption period is ten (10) days after sale in New Jersey;

— The redemption period is three (3) months after sale in Wyoming;

— The redemption time period is six (6) to nine (9) months after sale in Vermont, Illinois, South Dakota, Colorado, New Mexico, Arizona, Utah, Idaho and Oregon;

— The redemption time limit is one (1) year after sale in Maine, New Hampshire, Massachusetts, Kentucky, Alabama, Iowa, Arkansas, Missouri, Michigan, Wisconsin, Minnesota, Kansas, North Dakota, Montana, Washington, California, Nevada and Alaska;

— The redemption time limit is two (2) years after sale in Tennessee; and

— The redemption time limit is three (3) years after sale in Rhode Island.

[Legal Problem Solver. Reader's Digest, 1997; p. 239.] Consult a qualified attorney for specific information in the appropriate state or jurisdiction [and see, www.google.com/U.S.ForeclosureLaws].

Fifteen (15) Tips for Avoiding Foreclosure

Foreclosures and deficiency judgments could severely affect the consumer's creditworthiness, and therefore, serious efforts should be made to avoid foreclosure (see Chapter Three: "Credit Bureaus, Credit Scores and the Credit Business," *supra*). Fifteen (15) tips to avoid foreclosure follow:

1. Be engaged. Losing your home or other real estate can be distressing, and even depressing. Do not ignore this problem. Be engaged. The further behind the consumer gets in his or her mortgage payments, the more difficult it becomes to reinstate the loan, and the more likely the consumer will lose the property.

2. Contact the lender promptly upon realizing that you have a payment problem. Believe it or not, legitimate lenders do not

want your house. What they want is the money they expected to earn from granting the mortgage to the consumer. Many lenders have options for the consumer to help them through difficult times.

These options can include, for example:

(a) "The President's Making Home Affordable Plan;"
(b) Refinancing of the mortgage loan;
(c) Forbearance;
(d) Repayment plans; and
(e) Loan modifications.

3. <u>Do not hide your head in the sand</u>. Open and respond to all mail; e-mails, and other correspondence from the lender. Failure to be informed by your lender, and to respond to correspondence, will not be an excuse in foreclosure proceedings. Usually, the first notices the consumer receives will provide useful information about foreclosure prevention options and efforts that may assist the consumer. Subsequent correspondence may include important and informative notices of pending legal action.

4. <u>If you cannot afford your home, and particularly if you are behind in mortgage payments, try to sell it. Or, rent your home.</u> Enough said?

5. <u>Alternative, and/or in conjunction with 4 *supra*, always try to renegotiate the mortgage payment. Do not give up on this effort until the final chapter: foreclosure and sale.</u> Why not? All you have to lose is your home.

6. <u>Be knowledgeable. Know your mortgage rights</u>. Keep track of your mortgage loan documents and study them carefully. Be aware of your rights under the agreement, and what your lender (mortgagor) can lawfully do if you cannot make your payments.

    Learn about the foreclosure laws, procedures, and timeframes in your state and locale. Every state has its own foreclosure laws, procedures, and timeframes. Seek advice and assistance from competent sources.

7. <u>Make sure you understand the available foreclosure prevention options</u>. Another name for foreclosure prevention options is **"loss mitigation."** A good internet site for this information, among other sources is: www.fha.gov/foreclosure/index.cfm.
8. <u>Contact a knowledgeable attorney for advice and consultation</u>. Always a good practice. A simple telephone call to a knowledgeable attorney could, in many instances, save the consumer's home.
9. <u>Telephone or otherwise contact a HUD-approved housing counselor for consultation and advice</u>. The U.S. Department of Housing and Urban Development (HUD) funds free or very low cost housing counseling nationwide. Housing counselors can help the consumer understand the law and his or her options, organize their finances and represent them in negotiations with their lender if they need this assistance. Find a HUD-approved housing counselor near you or call (800) 569-4287 or TTY (800) 877-8339.
10. <u>Engage in debt and spending management</u>. You are in a financial crisis. Act like it. Prioritize your spending. After healthcare, at least for most of us, saving our home should be our first priority. The consumer should review his or her finances and determine where they can cut spending in order to make their mortgage payment. If necessary, delay payments on credit cards and other "unsecured" debt until you have paid your mortgage.

    Or, of course, try to lawfully increase your income with full or part-time employment opportunities.
11. <u>Demonstrate to the lender that you are serious about keeping your home. Use your assets</u>. Do you have assets—a second car, jewelry, a whole life insurance policy—that you can sell for cash to help pay your loan? Can anyone in your household get an extra job to bring in additional income? Even if these efforts don't significantly increase your available cash or your income, they demonstrate to your lender that you are willing to make sacrifices to keep your home.

12. Remember the words, **"produce the note!"** If the lender is to proceed successfully to foreclosure and sale, it must produce the note on the property.

13. Be very careful, and indeed wary, of so-called foreclosure prevention companies. Instead, follow the advice given in these fifteen (15) tips. Consult competent legal counsel and/or other qualified professional assistance that does not require hefty fees and costs.

    You don't need to pay fees for foreclosure prevention help—use that money to pay the mortgage instead. Many for-profit companies will contact you promising to negotiate with your lender. While these may be legitimate businesses, they will charge you a hefty fee (often two or three month's mortgage payment) for information and services your lender or a HUD-approved housing counselor will provide free if you contact them.

14. Avoid foreclosure recovery scams and schemes. Seek counsel from a competent professional, such as a lawyer or HUD-approved housing counselor, before hiring a so-called "foreclosure" expert or firm.

15. Attempt Redemption. See, "Redemption After Foreclosure," (xvii), *supra*. The consumer should remember that foreclosure is a costly and time-consuming process for lenders, thus providing incentives for the lender to avoid foreclosure.

With effort from the consumer, in most instances foreclosure can be avoided.

BANKRUPTCY 101

Capitalism without bankruptcy is like Christianity without hell.
-Frank Frederick Borman, II (former NASA astronaut)

I am including a brief discussion on bankruptcy in this chapter on avoiding foreclosure since, all too often, homeowners frequently raise the issue of possible bankruptcy when considering ways to save their home from foreclosure.

It is true that when a consumer is facing foreclosure on their home bankruptcy might be able to help.

In some cases, filing Chapter 7 bankruptcy can delay the foreclosure by a few months. In other cases, consumers have been known to save their home by filing for Chapter 13 bankruptcy repayment protection.

However, the consumer should be aware that bankruptcy is a very serious remedy with long-term repercussions for the consumer's credit. Expert consultation and careful consideration should be had by the consumer before declaring bankruptcy.

So, which looks better on your credit report? Foreclosure or Bankruptcy. It really does depend upon the consumer's specific circumstances. Ordinarily, a bankruptcy will remain on your credit report for 10 years, whereas a foreclosure will only remain on your report for 7 years. However, this difference does not necessarily conclude that foreclosure is the better choice. Understandably, mortgage lenders take foreclosures very seriously since their business is loaning money for people to buy homes. Therefore, these lenders will likely view a foreclosure more seriously than they will a bankruptcy that does not include a home loan.

Also, please see discussion of the "Short Sale" and the "Deed in lie of Foreclosure" earlier in this chapter.

Bankruptcy Fundamentals

Bankruptcy is a legal process in the United States that is governed and operated under Federal Law, Title 11 of the United States Code. Bankruptcy is a Federal remedy for debtors to cope with overwhelming debt; to assist individuals and businesses to shed their debt or to organize repayment of their debt under the protection of the bankruptcy court.

In short, there are three (3) types of bankruptcy proceedings:

— <u>Chapter 7 Bankruptcy</u> allows individual and business debtors to eliminate many of their debts in exchange for allowing their nonexempt property or assets to be sold to repay creditors. Chapter 7 Bankruptcy is commonly known as "straight" bankruptcy.

— <u>Chapter 11 Bankruptcy</u> is restricted to companies and allows them to reorganize their debts to remain in business. Chapter 11 Bankruptcy is frequently called "bankruptcy reorganization".

— <u>Chapter 13 Bankruptcy</u> is restricted to individual debtors and allows them to keep all of their property and arrange a repayment plan. Chapter 13 Bankruptcy is frequently known as "company reorganization" to pay part or all of their debts over a maximum three to five years period.

Some Bankruptcy Tips and Secrets

1. It is true that Chapter 7 Bankruptcy eliminates debts, but it does not necessarily eliminate all debts. For instance, Chapter 7 bankruptcy does not as a rule eliminate (i) child support, (ii) alimony, (ii) most tax debts, (iv) most student loans, (v) and most secured debts. These debts are called <u>exemptions</u> to Chapter 17 bankruptcy.

2. In some situations, Chapter 13 bankruptcy can be helpful in reducing or even eliminating under a repayment plan the exemptions to Chapter 7 bankruptcy in 1 above.

3. Even in Chapter 13 bankruptcy, unsecured debts such as credit card debt that remains after the repayment plan is complete will be discharged (wiped out).

4. Bankruptcy can delay the process but it cannot stop completely a creditor's repossession of secured property such as houses, cars, etc.

5. Beware that Chapter 7, 11 and 13 bankruptcy usually will not eliminate the so-called "nondischargeable" debts:

(i)   debts the debtor forgot or simply failed to list in his or her bankruptcy petition documents; unless the creditor learns of the bankruptcy in time to participate;

(ii) debts for personal injury or wrongful death caused by the wrongful acts (intoxicated driving, for example) of the debtor; and

(iii) fines and penalties imposed against the debtor for violating the law, such as traffic tickets and criminal restitution.

The basics of the effects of bankruptcy on foreclosure are as follows:

(1)   The Automatic Stay: Delaying Foreclosure.

When the homeowner files a Chapter 7 or a Chapter 13 bankruptcy action with the local U.S. Bankruptcy Court, the court automatically issues a court order, called the Order for Relief, which imposes immediately an "automatic stay" of the foreclosure.

This bankruptcy court-ordered "automatic stay" orders all of the homeowner's (bankruptcy petitioner's) creditors to stop trying to collect monies from the homeowner immediately. Therefore, if the homeowner's home is scheduled for a foreclosure sale, the scheduled foreclosure is immediately postponed indefinitely while the bankruptcy action is pending. This process can ordinarily take at least 3 or four months.

This short-term "stay" or delay can help the homeowner's attempt to re-group, catch a breath, etc.

(2)   There are, however, two important exceptions to the "automatic stay" delay of foreclosure:

(i)   Motion to Lift Stay.

The creditor (or lender, or mortgagor) may file with the bankruptcy court in the homeowner's bankruptcy case a "motion to lift stay", asking permission of the bankruptcy judge to allow the creditor to continue with the foreclosure sale. The judge may or may not order the stay; but typically, depending a lot upon how soon the creditor files the motion to lift the stay, the homeowner could get less time before final foreclosure.

(ii) Foreclosure Notice Previously Filed.

In several states, such as California for example, a bankruptcy "automatic stay" will not toll (stop the clock) on the advance or previous notice of a foreclosure. In other words, some states require the lender to give the homeowner at least three month's or so notice before filing for foreclosure. Therefore, if the homeowner receives a 3-month notice of default (before foreclosure), and then files for bankruptcy after two months (for example) have passed, the 3-month period would expire after the homeowner has been in bankruptcy for only one month. At the time the lender could file a motion to lift the stay and ask petition the bankruptcy judge to allow them to schedule the foreclosure sale.

(3) The Miracle of Chapter 13 Bankruptcy in Avoiding Foreclosure

Generally, people love their homes.

Consequently, there are many homeowners who will do whatever it legally takes to stay in their homes for as long as possible. It is commonly believed that when the homeowner is behind on mortgage payments and there seems to be little to no hope of catching up, one of the best strategies to stay in the home longer is to file a Chapter 13 bankruptcy petition.

Essentially, what Chapter 13 bankruptcy does is allow the homeowner to make back payments (pay off what is called the "arrearage" or late, or unpaid payments) over a repayment period of time. This repayment period of time is usually no more than about 5 years.

But, as expected, there's a catch. The homeowner must have enough income during this repayment period of time (i) to at least stay current with mortgage payments (ii) while simultaneously remaining up to date with the arrearage payments. Staying current with these and other commitments of the Chapter 13 bankruptcy repayment plan will cause the homeowner to forestall foreclosure and hold on to their home.

(4) <u>Chapter 13 Bankruptcy and Multiple (2nd and 3rd) Mortgage</u>
    <u>Payments</u>

Second and Third Mortgage Payments on the home could also be eliminated with the assistance of a Chapter 13 bankruptcy filing and repayment plan.

As an example, if the homeowner's first mortgage is secured by the entire value of the house, the homeowner could no longer have any value or equity in the property to secure subsequent mortgages. This scenario is very possible in this market where many homes have decreased in value.

In such a case as described above, the Chapter 13 bankruptcy court could remove the second, third, etc., mortgages as secured debt and recategorize these mortgages as unsecured debt. This is a good thing for the homeowner because, under Chapter 13 bankruptcy, Unsecured debt always gets last priority in payment and frequently does not require payment.

Bankruptcy Criminal Penalties

There are some bankruptcy actions that could result in criminal sanctions against the debtor, including imprisonment. For example, the bankruptcy debtor could face criminal charges and possibly go to jail for:

(1) Defrauding (in effect, stealing from) tenants;
(2) Forging a bankruptcy judge's signature;
(3) Committing perjury (lying under oath) during the creditor's meeting, among other acts.

<u>Summary</u>: Chapter Four-Fifteen (15) Tips for Avoiding Foreclosure

1. Remember the phrase "Produce the note" when facing foreclosure. The lender must produce it in order to complete the foreclosure. Consult a qualified attorney or other professional about this issue.

2. Some experts have predicted or assessed that upwards of forty percent (40%) of mortgage notes cannot be produced by the mortgagor or lender upon demand.

3. Nationwide, courts generally have responded favorably to the "produce the note" strategy.

4. Beware of tax consequences with the "short sale" as well as the "deed in lieu of foreclosure"

5. With effort from the consumer, in most instances foreclosure can be avoided.

6. The law requires that the lender send the consumer a formal "Notice of Default" prior to taking any further foreclosure action against the consumer.

7. After receiving a "Notice of Default," if the consumer pays the full amount owed on the mortgage within the specified time limit, and then continues timely payments, the lender is prohibited by law from taking further action against the consumer.

8. Many states allow a "period of redemption after foreclosure and sale" in which the consumer has the opportunity to redeem their home and buy it back.

9. Believe it or not, legitimate lenders do not want your house. Too much trouble; not their business. Many lenders, therefore, have options for consumers to help them through difficult financial times. Foreclosing on your house can be quite problematic for the lender.

10. Foreclosure scams and schemes are numerous in our society. Avoid them. Contact a lawyer or other qualified housing professional for advice prior to getting involved with so-called foreclosure prevention companies or foreclosure recovery scams and schemes.

11. Bankruptcy can delay the process but it cannot stop completely a creditor's repossession of secured property such as houses, cars, etc.

12. However, bankruptcy (particularly Chapter 7 bankruptcy) can be very helpful in wiping out credit card debt and other unsecured debt.

Chapter Five

Avoiding Identity Theft
and Identity Fraud

Worldwide, identity theft is so bad that it has officially hit the comedy circuit:

> "An identity thief who has stolen over half a million identities over the past two years returned all but four of them, declaring the identities 'totally worthless' and 'an enormous waste of time and hard work." [www.fool. com]

Identity theft is no joke. Neither is identity fraud. Both are very serious crimes.

In its recent reports, the United States Federal Trade Commission estimates that as many as 9 million or more American citizens have their identities stolen each year. In other words, the likelihood is high that either you or someone you know has experienced some form of identity theft or identity fraud [www.ftc.gov/bcp].

Identity theft and identity fraud take many forms. Thieves of your identity may rent an apartment, obtain a credit card, or establish a utility account (such as telephone, electric, et al.) in the consumer victim's name. All too frequently the victim does not find out about the theft of his or her identity until they reviewed their credit report or credit card statement, or until they are contacted by the dreaded debt collector.

Some identity theft and identity fraud victims are able to resolve their problems relatively quickly. Others, however, may need to spend hundreds, and even thousands, of dollars and considerable time (in days) trying to repair the serious damage done to their credit record and their good name.

I am aware of many consumers who have been victimized by identity theft and identity fraud who have lost out on employment opportunities. Others have been denied loans for housing, cars, and education due to the falsely negative information on their credit reports. I have even represented a few people who were falsely arrested for crimes they did not commit because of identity theft or identity fraud.

With enough identifying information about an individual, a criminal can take over that individual's identity to conduct a wide range of crimes: for example, false applications for loans and credit cards, fraudulent withdrawals from bank accounts, fraudulent use of telephone calling cards, or obtaining other goods or privileges which the criminal might be denied if he were to use her or his real name.

Further, if the criminal takes steps to ensure that bills for the falsely obtained credit cards, or bank statements showing the unauthorized withdrawals are sent to an address other than the victim's the victim may not become aware of what is happening until the criminal has already inflicted substantial damage on the victim's assets, credit, and reputation.

What are Identity Theft and Identity Fraud?

The terms "identity theft" and "identity fraud" are used interchangeably, but both are crimes. These terms refer to all types of crimes in which someone (the perpetrator) wrongfully obtains and uses another individual's personal data in some way that involves economic gain by deception or fraud [www.justice.gov/criminal].

Unlike fingerprints, which are unique to each person and cannot be given away to some other person for their use, an individual's personal data—including their Social Security number, bank account number, credit card number, telephone calling card number, and other valuable identification data—can be used to personally profit at the victim's expense, if they fall in the wrong hands.

What are the Most Common Ways for Thieves to Commit Identity Theft or Fraud?

Criminals can fairly easily steal your personal data without having to break into your home, office, or car:

TEN (10) MOST COMMON SCHEMES

1. "Shoulder surfing" is popular. This occurs when, in public places, for example, criminals watch you from a nearby location or you punch-in your telephone calling card number, or your credit card number, or they listen-in on your conversation if you give your credit card number over the telephone to a hotel, rental car company, et al.

2. "Dumpster diving" is a time-tested way of invading your privacy and stealing your identity. Investigative reporters, private investigators, law enforcement officers, and others, including criminals, have engaged in it for many years. The perpetrators go through your garbage cans, trash bins, commercial dumpsters, etc., and obtain copies of your checks, credit card and bank statements, and other personal records that typically carry your name, address, telephone numbers, Social Security numbers, and other pertinent information.

   These types of personal records make it much easier for criminals to gain control over accounts in your name and steal your identity.

3. "Skimming" usually occurs in restaurants and retail outlets. Criminals will steal your credit and debit card numbers by using a special storage device (for these valuable numbers) when processing your card.

4. "Phishing" occurs frequently when criminals pretend to be financial institutions or companies and send spam or pop-up

messages over the Internet to you to get you to reveal your personal information.

5. "<u>Changing your address</u>." Criminals will divert your billing statements to another location of their choosing by completing a change of address form (see, 8 <u>below</u>).

6. "<u>Common Stealing</u>" for criminals is not out of fashion in this electronic age. Thieves steal purses and wallets; your mail, including bank and credit card statements; "pre-approved" credit card offers and other "pre-approved" enticements using the customer's personal information; as well as your new bank checks or even your tax information (see, 8 <u>below</u>).

7. "<u>Employee Record Theft</u>." Criminals often steal consumers' employment or personnel records, as well as bribe other employees who have access to these records.

8. "<u>Pre-approved</u>" credit cards are a huge target for identity thieves. When the consumer receives applications for "pre-approved" credit cards in the mail, he or she may be very alert to (<u>if</u> discarding them) tear up the enclosed materials as well as the cards. Thieves could retrieve the cards and the materials and attempt to activate the credit cards for their own use without the consumer's knowledge.

9. "<u>Pretexting</u>" is popular among private investigators and law enforcement officers, as well as various security personnel. Pretexting, in sum, is lying. Criminals will use "pretexting" (false pretenses, or lying) to obtain the consumer's personal information from financial institutions.

10. "<u>Spamming</u>" is very similar to "phishing" (4, <u>above</u>). More so than "phishing," spamming tends to take advantage of the consumer's haste to explore the exciting features of the Internet. Many consumers respond to "spam" (unsolicited e-mail) that usually promises some benefit (free trips, laptop computer, <u>et al</u>.) but requests the consumer's identifying personal information. In many cases, the requester has no intention of keeping his or her promise.

Twenty (20) Steps To Avoid Becoming A Victim of Identity Theft and Identity Fraud

1. Keep uppermost in your mind the words "SCAM" and "SCHEME."

2. Be miserly, parsimonious . . . indeed, stingy . . . about giving out your personal information to others. Make sure you have reasons to trust others prior to giving out your personal information, at all times and regardless of where you are.

3. Adopt a "need to know" approach to revealing your personal information.

   Be cautious about the personal information you have printed on your personal bank checks. For example, do not include your Social Security and/or home telephone number on your bank checks. Your credit card company may need to know your mother's maiden name so that it can verify your identity when you call them to ask about your account. But, these and other personal questions should not be answered, or should raise the consumer's suspicion, when someone calls the consumer.

4. If a stranger (simply put: someone you do not know personally) contacts you either on the telephone, via email or mail, or otherwise, and offers you the chance to receive anything (i.e., a "major" credit card, an enticing prize, or other valuable item), but asks you for personal information such as your Social Security number, credit card number, mother's name, and so forth, request that they send you a printed or written application form.

5. If the requester, 4 above, will not comply, that is a bad sign. Inform them that you are not interested, and promptly end the conversation.

6. If the requester complies with what you are asking, 4 above, review the information, application, and their "pitch" to you very carefully. Make sure the financial institution or company your personal information is going to is reputable. Contact the Better Business Bureau (BBB) to inquire if any complaints have been filed against the firm.

7.   When traveling, have your mail held at your local post office, or ask a trusted family member, friend, or neighbor to collect and hold your mail while you are traveling.

8.   When traveling, try to use the telephone in a less public location; particularly when you need to relay personal financial information over the telephone.

9.   Check on all of your personal financial information on a regular basis. Look for what belongs, and what does not belong in your information.

10. Regarding your bank accounts or credit card accounts, make sure you are receiving monthly statements or reports that itemize transactions for the most recent months or reporting period.

11. If you are not receiving monthly statements or regular reporting period statements for the credit card or bank accounts you know you have, something is wrong. Call the appropriate financial institution or credit card company as quickly as possible and ask about it.

12. Be wary of your financial statements or financial reports being mailed to an address you have not explicitly and/or expressly authorized. Correct this situation with the appropriate financial institution or credit card representative immediately.

13. Always ask for financial statements or reports on you that you have not received; particularly more recent missing statements. Look for theft or fraud.

14. Do not just "glance" at your monthly financial statements or reports. Look at them carefully to determine whether some or all of your debt or charge transactions are real or fraudulent.

15. If you have reason to believe that someone has invaded, tampered with, or illegally used your personal information—via mail, e-mail, or otherwise—contact your appropriate financial institution or credit card company immediately to report your concerns and to request further action.

16. Acquire and review periodically a copy of your FICO credit report. Remember, you are entitled to at least one (1) <u>free</u> annual credit report (See, Chapter Three: "Credit Bureaus, Credit Scores and the Credit Business," <u>supra</u>, para. 17, under

"A Summary of Major Consumer Rights Under the Fair Credit Reporting Act (FCRA)").

You can order your free annual credit report online at annualcreditreport.com, or by calling 1-877-322-8228, or by competing the Annual Credit Report Request Form and mailing it to:

Annual Credit Report Request Service
P.O. Box 105281
Atlanta, Georgia 30348-5281

When you order your free annual credit report, be prepared to provide pertinent data such as your name, address, Social Security number, and date of birth.

17. A customarily-prepared FICO credit report usually includes a list of all bank and financial accounts under the consumer's name, and other information useful in determining whether someone has unlawfully opened or used any accounts using your identity.
18. Gather and maintain careful records of your personal financial and banking accounts.
19. I recommend that the consumer collect and retain his or her monthly or periodic financial statements and checks for at lest 3 years (for identity theft purposes). Many experts advise that you retain these statements and checks for at least one year. Most financial institutions are required to maintain copies of your checks, debt transactions, and similar transactions for 5 years (usually on microfilm, cd, etc.). However, these institutions will usually charge you for developing and producing copies of your financial transactions.

The bottom line is this: If the need arises for the consumer to dispute a particular check or transaction, particularly if the check or transaction purports to bear the consumer's signatures, the consumer's own (preferably original) records will be more immediately accessible and more useful to the institutions the consumer has contacted for clarification and so forth.

20. Do not leave personal financial data in mobile objects such as cars, motorcycles, planes, busses, trucks, etc. These financial records (such as credit card receipts, car rental agreements, copies of credit cards, etc.) may be found by some individual who decides to use your information for criminal purposes.

Be Aware Of What Criminals Do With Your Stolen Identity: Five (5) Points

Once they have stolen your identity criminals can use it in a number of ways. They can:

1. Engage in Credit Card fraud, by—

    (i) Opening new credit card accounts in your name. They then use the cards and do not pay the credit card bills. The delinquency then appears on your credit report;
    (ii) Changing the billing address on your credit card so that you no longer receive the bills. They run up charges on your credit card account. Because of the fraudulent billing address, it may be a long time before you realize there is a problem with your account.

2. Engage in Bank and Finance fraud, by—

    (i) Creating counterfeit checks using your name and account number;
    (ii) Opening a bank account in your name and writing bad checks;
    (iii) Cloning (duplicating) your ATM or debit card and making electronic withdrawals, and draining your accounts;
    (iv) Taking out a loan using your identity.

3. Engage in Telephone and Utilities fraud, by—

    (i) Opening a new phone or wireless account in your name, or run up charges on your existing account; and
    (ii) Using your identity to secure utility services such as electricity, heating, or cable television.

4. Engage in Government Documents fraud, by—

    (i) Acquiring a driver's license, passport, or other official identification card issued in your name but with their picture;
    (ii) Using your name and Social Security number to get government benefits; and
    (iii) Filing fraudulent tax returns using your information.

5. Engage in Other fraud, by—

    (i) Gaining employment (getting a job) using the consumer's Social Security number;
    (ii) Renting a house or apartment, or securing medical services using the consumer's name; and
    (iii) Giving <u>your</u> personal information to police during an arrest. When these criminals do not show up for their court dates, warrants are issued by the Court for arrests in your name.

<u>What To Do If You Have Become A Victim Of Identity Theft Or Identity Fraud</u>

1. Immediately upon realizing or believing that he or she has become a victim of identity theft or fraud, the consumer should <u>act</u> to minimize the damages to their personal funds and financial accounts, as well as their reputation.
2. <u>Identity Theft and Assumption Deterrence Act (of 1998)</u>. This Act gives authority to both the United States Department of Justice and the United States Federal Trade Commission to

receive and prosecute cases of identity theft and fraud. The Department of Justice (DOJ) further prosecutes cases of identity fraud and theft under a variety of other federal statutes.

The Federal Trade Commission (FTC) is responsible for receiving and processing complaints from consumers who believe they may be victims of identity theft, providing information materials to them. The Commission (FTC) further refers those consumer complaints to the appropriate agencies and institutions, including the "Big 3" major credit reporting agencies and law enforcement agencies such as the Department of Justice (DOJ).

The Department of Justice (DOJ) prosecutorial abilities include not only its many legal divisions such as the Civil Division and Criminal Division, but the numerous United States Attorneys' offices throughout the 50 states and the District of Columbia, et al. [www.justice.gov/criminal/fraud].

The Identity Theft and Assumption Deterrence Act (ITADA) of 1998 crated a new office of identity theft, which prohibits knowingly transfer[ring] or us[ing], without lawful authority, a means of identification of another person with the intent to commit, or to aid or abet, any unlawful activity that constitutes a violation of Federal law, or that constitutes a felony under any applicable State or local law [18 U.S.C. § 1028(a)(7)]. This offense, in most circumstances, carries a maximum term of 15 years' imprisonment, a fine, and criminal forfeiture of any personal property used or intended to be used to commit the offense.

3. Other Federal Identity Theft and Identity Fraud Laws. Schemes to commit identity theft or fraud may also involve violations of other statutes such as identification fraud (18 U.S.C. § 1028), credit card fraud (18 U.S.C. § 1029), computer fraud (18 U.S.C. § 1030), mail fraud (18 U.S.C. § 1341), wire fraud (18 U.S.C. § 1343) or financial institution fraud (18 U.S.C. § 1344). Each of these federal offenses are felonies that carry substantial penalties; in some cases, as high as 30 years imprisonment, fines, and criminal forfeiture.

4. Depending upon the Identity Theft or Identity Fraud alleged by the consumer, the following are just some of the agencies and institutions that may be contacted by the consumer victim:

(i) The Federal Trade Commission (FTC). Contact the Federal Trade Commission (FTC) to report the situation, whether online (www.ftc.gov/bcp); by telephone toll-free at 1-877-ID THEFT (877-438-4338) or TDD at 202-326-2502, or by mail to Consumer Response Center, FTC, 600 Pennsylvania Avenue, N.W., Washington, DC 20580.

(ii) The Department of Justice (DOJ) online (www.justice.gov/criminal) headquarters in Washington, DC, or contact your nearest U.S. Attorney's Office in your state.

(iii) The Federal Bureau of Investigation (FBI). Contact your nearest FBI office in your state.

(iv) The United States Secret Service, (USSS) Washington, DC; or your nearest Secret Service office.

(v) The United States Postal Inspection Service, (USPIS). Contact your local post office for the correct contact information, when your identity theft problem involves theft of mail, change-of-address form problems, etc.

(vi) The Federal Deposit Insurance Corporation (FDIC). Contact regarding FDIC-insured banks headquartered in Washington, DC.

(vii) The Social Security Administration (SSA). When you suspect that your Social Security number is being fraudulently used. Telephone: 1-800-269-0271 to report.

(viii) The Internal Revenue Service (IRS). When you suspect or believe the improper use of identification data is connected with tax violations. Telephone: 1-800-829-0433 to report.

The "Big 3" Credit Reporting Agencies

(ix) Equifax:

— To report fraud, call 1-800-525-6285 or write to P.O. Box 740250, Atlanta, GA 30374-0250;
— To order a copy of your credit report ($8 in most states), write to P. O. Box 740241, Atlanta, GA 30374-0241, or call 1-800-685-1111.
— To dispute information in your report, call the phone number provided on your credit report; and
— To opt out for pre-approved offers of credit, call 1-888-567-8688 or write to Equifax Options, P.O. Box 740123, Atlanta, GA 30374-0123.

(x) Experian (formerly TRW):

— To report fraud, call 1-888-EXPERIAN or 1-888-397-3742, fax to 1-800-301-7196, or write to P.O. Box 1017, Allen, TX 75013;
— To order a copy of your credit report ($8 in most states); P.O. Box 2104, Allen, TX 75013, or call 1-8888-EXPERIAN.
— To dispute information in your report, call the phone number provided on your credit report; and
— To opt out of pre-approved offers of credit and marketing lists, call 1-800-353-0809 or 1-800-5OPTOUT or write to P.O. Box 919, Allen, TX 75013.

(xi) TransUnion:

— To report fraud, call 1-800-680-7289 or write to P.O. Box 6790, Fullerton, CA 92634;
— To order a copy of your credit report ($8 in most states), write to P.O. Box 390, Springfield, PA 19064 or call 1-800-888-4213;

— To dispute information in your report, call the phone number provided on your credit report; and

— To opt out of pre-approved offers of credit and marketing lists, call 1-800-680-7293 or 1-888-5OPTOUT or write to P.O. Box 97328, Jackson, MS 39238.

(xii) **Check Verification**. Contact the major "check verification" companies if you believe you have had checks stolen or bank accounts set up by identity thieves. The <u>California Public Interest Research Group (CalPIRG)-Privacy Rights Clearinghouse</u>, for example, provides a good list of check verification firms. Some of these companies that merchants use include:

(1) CheckRite (1-800-766-2748)
(2) ChexSystems (1-800-428-9623). Closed checking accounts.
(3) CrossCheck (1-800-552-1900)
(4) Equifax (1-800-437-5120)
(5) NPC or National Processing Company (1-800-526-5380)
(6) SCAN (1-800-262-7771)
(7) TeleCheck (1-800-710-9898)

(xiii) **Financial Institutions.** Contact all banks, credit unions and other financial institutions you have accounts with that an identity thief has taken control over that have been created in your name (with your identity) without your knowledge. It is possible that you may need to cancel those accounts, place stop-payment orders on any outstanding checks that may not have cleared, change your ATM (Automated Teller Machine) cards, account, and your PIN (Personal Identification Number).

(xiv) **Creditors.** Contact all creditors with whom your name or identifying data have been fraudulently used. This includes, for example, your long-distance telephone company if your long-distance calling card has been stolen or you find questionable or fraudulent charges on your bill.

Summary: Chapter Five—Avoiding Identity Theft and Identity Fraud

1. Adopt a "need to know" approach to revealing your personal information. Be stingy about giving out your personal information to others in any form, manner, or fashion.
2. Check on all of your personal financial information on a regular basis, including credit reports, bank statements, credit card statements, and so forth. Do not just "glance" at these documents or this information; review it carefully.
3. For identity theft purposes, I recommend the consumer collect and retain his or her monthly financial statements and checks for at least 3 years.

Chapter Six

Work-At-Home Scams and Schemes [Employment]

Caution: Scam Alert!

Hello, my name is John Doe:

A little about myself . . . I'm 40 years old, and I live in Delaware. I've been working at home and making a living at it since 2006. I've been able to earn a great income while enjoying being in the comfort of my own home. I'm saving money on gas and I sure don't miss sitting in traffic. As I now write my own pay checks, I don't have to worry about my job security anymore. Best of all, I can now spend more time than ever with my two daughters.

Four years ago after I got laid-off, I was also searching for work at home opportunities on the internet. I was absolutely shocked at the number of scams out there that required 0 fees upfront and provided outdated information with weak customer service (if any).

I spent nearly 3 months trying almost every work at home opportunity on the entire internet; from data entry to processing rebates to simply typing at home and everything in between. I was scammed by all kinds of "work at home programs" and I lost a bunch of money. I was in the position where I had to create an income quick, I had no other choice. Even though I thought that most of these programs were probably scams, I tried them anyway because I knew that if just one of them worked for me, that's all it would take to put an end to my financial difficulties.

The general rule I have found about work at home programs is that if it sounds too good to be true, it probably is. We've all seen the ads that promise you will make millions online without doing any work. These types of ads fool consumers by making big promises that don't deliver. Think about it twice before sending your hard earned money to these crooks.

Of all the opportunities that I tried, most were complete scams that just took my money. However, I did find two work at home programs that actually work. I'll give you an honest review about the two programs that work. If you're looking at any other program besides these two, you are most likely wasting your time. After trying so many, these are the only two that worked for me.

Don't Get Scammed and Good Luck!

John Doe

[Letter from the Inter, 01-27-2010, <u>Consumer Alert</u>]
It, too, is a scam!

Avoiding work-at-home scams and schemes is actually not as difficult as it may seem. But, the consumer must use common sense, repress the "speed-to-greed", and do his or her research on the proposed "opportunity" to make a lot of money. If the "opportunity" sounds too good to be true . . . it usually is too good to be true [www.consumerfraudreporting.org; www.work-at-home-site.com; www.ftc.gov].

Most "work-at-home" scams and schemes are generally run by so-called "information brokers." These schemes target people who, for whatever reason, desire to make money from the convenience and comfort of their own place of living (their home). Victims of "work-at-home" scams and schemes are promised a lot of money for their efforts, but almost invariably are disappointed with the results.

These scams and schemes do well because there are a lot of people who need money to live, or want extra money, and many of them are intrigued by the prospect or promise of getting money "the easy way."

Work-at-home job postings are commonplace. Employment listings for multi-level marketing positions, research jobs, data entry positions, paid surveys, envelope stuffing, product assembly, medical billing, vending machine and display rack businesses, and a number of other ways to allegedly make a lot of money fast are everywhere.

"Work-at-Home" Scams To Avoid

The current consensus is that consumers should avoid generally the following "work-at-home" scams and schemes, among others:

Typing & Data Entry "Jobs" Scam	Derby House Fabrics Bookkeeper Job Scam
Cashing Fake Checks & Wire Transfer Scams	Recruitment Offer Scam By Apex Paperworks
Package Forwarding & Reshipping Job Scam	Part Time Job Offer Scam—WUJIANG TEXTILE CO. LTD.
Google Money / Work At Home Scams	Infomercial Scams
Paid Surveys Online Scams	Job Offer 10% Get Back If Interested

Warning: Government Cash Grant Scams	Company Representative Needed (Payment For Services)
Rebate Processors Scams	Universal Fabrics and Fashion Inc. Job Opportunity
Cash Gifting—Giving Programs Scams	Receivables Processing Specialist
Cash4Gold.com Scams	IRS Tax Refund Scam Email
Work At Home Sites Busted By FTC	Bookkeeper Work At Home Medical Billing Scam
Top 5 Work At Home Scam Fighting Websites	UK National Lottery Online Promo
Top 5 Work At Home Scams	Lottery Scam

There are so many work-at-home scams and schemes out there that the National Consumers League ranks them in its list of "Top 10 Frauds" in the United States [www.nclnet.org; www.ftc.gov/opa; www.scambusters.org].

Just Say "No"

All too frequently, advertised "work-at-home" opportunities or positions are not what most people would consider to be real or legitimate jobs. Generally, there are no benefits, and no salary or hourly wages, but only promises to the victim of making money. What's worse is that frequently these so-called opportunities are allegedly so lucrative for the consumer victim that the scammer or schemer actually charges fees to the victim to give him or her the listings, and/or provide the victim with information on getting started, and/or to set up the alleged business.

The simple response to the question of whether the consumer should pay for work of any type, and particularly work-at-home "opportunities," is to just say "no." Despite what the job postings for work-at-home opportunities say or promise, remember this fact: **legitimate employers pay the employee, not the other way around.**

Too Good To Be True

A tried and true rule of thumb is: If the work-at-home opportunity sounds too good to be true, it usually is too good to be true. Just say "no."

The following are some examples of this "too good to be true" rule of thumb:

Stay home and get paid thousands.

— Earn $2,000 a day from home.
— Earn cash, stay home, enjoy life.
— Get paid cash daily via ATM.
— Work part-time from home. Earn cash.
— Earn $10K or more a month from home.
— High earnings from home with little or no effort.

Although difficult to do when in financial distress, the consumer should try to think logically, rationally and reasonably. Ordinarily, the chances of making legitimately a lot of money doing a minimal amount of work are simply not good. And crime doesn't pay. "Measure twice and cut once" (i.e., think twice, at least) before agreeing to any financial or commercial venture that sounds too good to be true. It usually is.

Investigate the Potential Employer

Because many "work-at-home" scammers and schemers are very clever and creative about advertising their alleged opportunities to the consumer, and since the goal is to make the victim believe that the so-called job opportunity is real, the consumer should research the potential employer if he or she is not sure about the company.

There are several sources to contact in researching these companies, but I recommend at least the following five (5) as investigation resources:

1. The United States Federal Trade commission (FTC). As former Special Counsel to the Chairman of the Federal Trade Commission, I can say with some confidence that the FTC works for the consumer to prevent fraudulent, deceptive, and unfair business practices in the American marketplace. This agency, through its Consumer Protection Bureau as well as its Bureau of Competition, also provides information to help consumers recognize, prohibit, and avoid fraud [see, http://www.ftc.gov, or call toll-free 1-877-382-4357].

2. The Better Business Bureau (BBB). Frequently the consumer can enter the name or website into the BBB search box on its website to find out whether there have been complaints against the company or firm, and whether the company or firm has an unsatisfactory record with the Bureau [see, http://www.bbb.org].

3. The United States Postal Inspection Service (USPIS). Every day, illegal "work-at-home" mail fraud scams and schemes, as well as other mail fraud scams and schemes separate consumer victims from heir hard-earned money. The consumer victim can contact his or her nearest U.S. Postal Inspector if any part of the scam or scheme involves the U.S. mail [see, 1-888-877-7644; http://www.uspsoig.gov/hotlinedefault.aspx].

4. The State Attorney General. In each state and the District of Columbia, the local State Attorney General has significant jurisdiction over consumer protection issues. Contact this office in your state with questions concerning "work-at-home" issues as well as other consumer issues [see, the National Association of Attorneys General, www.naag.org; and http:///www.globalcomputing.com/states.html].

5. The "Work-at-Home" Scams Bulletin Board. This bulletin board contains information and points of reference on work-at-home scams and schemes. Registered users on this site can post questions about scams and schemes [see, MLM/Pyramid Scams Bulletin Board].

6. The National Fraud Information Center (NFIC). The NFIC accepts reports about attempts to defraud consumers on the telephone or the Internet [www.fraud.org].

7. <u>The National Consumers League (NCL)</u>. Founded in 1899 the NCL is the oldest private, nonprofit consumer organization in the United States [www.naticonsumersleague.org].
8. <u>Cybercops</u> provide useful resources as well [www.cybercops.org].

<u>Summary</u>: Chapter Six— Work-at-Home Scams and Schemes

1. A general rule to remember is that real or legitimate employers pay the employee, <u>not</u> the other way around. If the consumer is asked to pay for work of any type, and particularly, work-at-home jobs, just say "no."
2. If the work-at-home opportunity sounds too good to be true, it usually is too good to be true.
3. Always investigate or research the potential work-at-home employers thoroughly. The Internet is a good research source for this type of background investigation.

Chapter Seven

From Charles Ponzi to Bernard Madoff: The "Ponzi" and Other Investment Schemes

CHARLES PONZI

Surprise. Charles Ponzi did <u>not</u> invent the investment scheme that was named after him: the "Ponzi."

In fact, decades before Charles Ponzi's birth, the famous writer Charles Dickens, in his 1857 novel, *Little Dorrit*, described a very similar scheme. Ponzi, however, raked in such incredible amounts of money using the technique in the 1920s, and became so well-known throughout the United States during that time, the scheme was named after him.

The notorious Charles Ponzi emigrated from Italy to the United States in 1903. His original scheme, in theory, was founded or based on the concept of arbitraging international reply coupons for postage stamps. In other words, he would simultaneously purchase and sell the same equivalent security (reply coupon for postage stamps) in order to profit from price discrepancies in postage. Soon, however, with his outrageous promises of huge profit returns to his investors, Ponzi began diverting investors' money to support payments to earlier investors and to his personal wealth ["Ponzi Schemes," <u>www. ssa.gov</u>; web.archive.org (2004)].

With his postage stamp speculation scheme in the 1920s, Charles Ponzi scammed thousands of New England residents. His pitch to investors was that he could take advantage of differences between United States and foreign currencies used to buy and sell international mail coupons. He convinced his investors that he could provide a 40% return in just 90 days time compared with just 5% interest on bank savings accounts. Ponzi was inundated with millions of dollars in funds from investors; and, notably, in one three-hour period of investor frenzy, he took in a million dollars—in the year 1921! [Dunn (2004), <u>Ponzi: The Incredible True Story of the King of Financial Cons</u>; Zuckoff (2005), <u>Ponzi's Scheme: The True Story of a Financial Legend</u>].

Eventually, though a few early-bird investors received the money promised to make the scheme appear legal, an investigation determined that Charles Ponzi had purchased only about $30 worth of international postage coupons [SEC, www.sec.gov].

BERNARD MADOFF

Bernard "Bernie" Madoff will for decades be known as the scammer who took the "Ponzi" scheme technique to the next high level. For perspective, consider the following: As a result of his almost 30-year Wall Street "Ponzi" scheme (i) the amount of money missing from Madoff's client accounts, including fabricated gains, was almost $65 billion; (ii) the court-appointed trustee estimated actual investor losses of $18 billion; and (iii) his criminal sentence in Federal Court on June 29, 2009 was 150 years in prison (the maximum allowed) and forfeiture of $170 billion! [Safer, Morley (September 27, 2009), "The Madoff Scam: Meet The Liquidator," www.cbsnews.com, <u>60 Minutes</u>; Bray Chad (March 12, 1009), "Madoff Pleads Guilty to Massive Fraud, "www.wsj.com, <u>The Wall Street Journal</u>; "Bernard Madoff gets 150 years behind bars for fraud scheme," www.cbc.ca, <u>CBS News</u> (2009); Healy, Jack (June 29, 2009), "Madoff Sentenced to 150 Years for Ponzi Scheme," www.nytimes.com, <u>The New York Times </u>(2009)].

Prior to his admission and conviction of running the largest "Ponzi" scheme in the history of the United States, Bernard Madoff was a former Chairman of the respected NASDAQ stock exchange and founder of the Wall Street firm Bernard L. Madoff Investment Securities LLC. The Madoff firm was one of the top market maker businesses on Wall Street. Before his final downfall, the U.S. Securities and Exchange Commission (SEC) had conducted several investigations into Madoff's business practices since 1992, which observers and critics argue were incompetently handled [Lieberman, Pallavi, Howard, McCoy, and Krantz (December 15, 2008), "Investors remain amazed over Madoff's sudden downfall," www.usatoday.com, USA Today (2008); O'Hara (1995), Market Microstructure Theory].

Bernard Madoff is, at the very least, the Charles Ponzi of this generation and of this century.

WHAT IS A "PONZI" SCHEME

A Ponzi scheme is a type of illegal pyramid scheme [www.sec.gov/answers/ponzi.htm]. It relies on the consumers' mistaken belief in a nonexistent financial reality, including the hope of an extremely high rate of return on their investment. In other words, it relies on greed.

The Ponzi scheme is one of the oldest and simplest forms of investment swindles, in which the victims' money is never invested in anything. Early investors are paid "gains" out of money put up by later investors, and the process continues until the bubble finally bursts [BBB and NASAA, Investor Alert (1988).] You could say that the typical Ponzi scheme operates on the "rob-Peter-to-pay-Paul" principle: money from new investors is used to pay off earlier investors until the entire scheme collapses. The later investors lose the monies they invested. In a Ponzi scheme, the schemer acts as a "hub" for the victims, interacting in some way with all of the other victims directly.

SIMILAR SCHEMES

1. The Pyramid scheme can be a form of fraud similar in some ways to a Ponzi scheme. It, too, relies upon a frequently mistaken

belief in a nonexistent or an extremely unreasonable financial reality. In this scheme, those individuals who recruit additional participants in the scheme benefit directly. In fact, failure by a participant to recruit new members usually means no investment return for the participant. In contrast with Ponzi schemes, which claim to rely on some esoteric investment approach such as insider connections and so forth, and tend to attract more well-to-do investors, the Pyramid scheme explicitly claim that new money will be the source of payouts for participants. Because of its structure, the Pyramid scheme usually crumbles faster than the Ponzi because the Pyramid requires exponential or large increases in participants to sustain itself. The Ponzi, on the other hand, can survive longer simply by persuading most existing participants to "reinvest" their money in the scheme, with a comparatively smaller number of new participants.

2. The Bubble scheme involves ever-rising and unsustainable prices in an open market. You have probably heard recently about the "Bubble" in housing or real estate prices. The Bubble can also exist in numerous other markets, including stocks, gambling, oil and gas, and so forth. Like the Ponzi and the Pyramid, the Bubble counts on the voluntary suspension of disbelief and the unrealistic expectation of large profits by the victim. As long as the buyers (be they homebuyers, stock buyers, or whatever) are willing and able to pay ever-increasing prices, sellers can get out with a good profit, and there does not even need to be a schemer behind a "Bubble." Often, Bubbles can rise or occur without any fraud whatsoever. Take, for example, the previously-stated bubble in housing prices in a local market that may rise sharply but eventually drop equally as sharply because of overbuilding. "Bubbles" are frequently said to be based upon the "greater fool" theory. If you believe the Austrian Business Cycle Theory, Bubbles are caused by expanding the money supply beyond what genuine capital investment will support. If this theory is true, "Bubbles" probably could quality as a Ponzi scheme, with expanded credit taking the place of an expanded pool of investors.

[The Austrian Business Cycle Theory (or "ABCT") is an explanation from the Austrian School of business and economics which describes regularly occurring booms and busts in the economy. It is sometimes called the "hangover theory" (Joseph T. Slaerno, <u>Austrian Economics Newsletter</u>, Fall 1996)].

3. The <u>"Robbing Peter to Pay Paul" Scheme</u>. As mentioned previously in this chapter, the typical Ponzi scheme operates generally on the "rob-Peter-to-pay-Paul" principle. But, every "rob-Peter-to-pay-Paul" scheme is not necessarily a Ponzi scheme. The scheme generally occurs when debts are due and the money to pay them is lacking whether because of bad luck or intentional theft. Debtors will often make their payments by borrowing or stealing from other investors they have.

HOW TO AVOID THE PONZI AND OTHER ILLEGAL INVESTMENT SCHEMES

There are several signs that should alert the investor to probable financial danger when considering an investment:

TEN (10) SIGNS

1. If the investment promises the investor a high rate of return that cannot be matched or equaled by any other legal investment, this is a danger sign. Remember: *If it sounds too good to be true, it probably is too good to be true.*

2. Is there a legitimate independent agency or institution which verifies the promised performance of the investment? If not, be careful.

3. Is the investment scheme properly registered with the proper authorities at the local, state, and federal levels (e.g., state insurance commissioner, Securities and Exchange Commission, etc.)? If not, do not invest in it.

4. Has the investment or the investment firm undergone a regulatory audit? Every investment and investment firm needs an audit.

5. Do you understand the full financial and management structure and operation of the investment or the investment firm? If not, be careful.

6. Do you know what the product or service is that you are investing your money in? If not, be wary. If you are not investing your money in a product or service, do not invest.

7. What other investments or investment firms, if any, are connected with your potential investment or investment firm? What do you know about them? Are they legitimate or legal?

8. Can the investment manager or investment firm provide you with independent and reputable references? If not, be very wary.

9. Has the investment manager or investment firm ever been involved in a legal dispute with any investors in the past or the present? If so, have them explain fully.

10. Are you and/or other investors super-impressed or blinded by the "reputation" of an investment manager? If so, become grounded and check out the individual(s) carefully.

SOME RESOURCES FOR CONSUMERS TO HELP AVOID PONZI-LIKE SCHEMES

Twenty-Five (25) Resources

1. The United States Federal Trade Commission (FTC), Consumer Protection Bureau.

2. The United States Department of Justice, including the Civil Division, as well as the U.S Attorneys Offices in the appropriate state (DOJ).

3. The United States Securities and Exchange Commission (SEC).

4. The Attorney Generals Offices in the appropriate state.

5. The United States Commodities Futures Trading Commission (CFTC).

6. The North American Securities Administrators Association (NASAA).

7. The Alliance for Investor Education (AIE).

8. The National Futures Association (NFA).
9. The Insurance Commission or Commissioner for the appropriate state.
10. The CFA Institute.
11. The Financial Planning Association (FPA).
12. The National Endowment for Financial Education (NEFE).
13. The Financial Publishers Association (FPA)
14. The Financial Industry Regulatory Authority (FINRA).
15. The Investor Protection Trust (IPT).
16. TomorrowsMoney.org/SIFMA Foundation.
17. http://www.Investoreducation.org.
18. The American Association of Individual Investors (AAII).
19. The Board of Governors of the Federal Reserve System (FRS).
20. Better Investing.org.
21. Investment Company Institute Education Foundation (ICIEF).
22. Council for Economic Education (CEE).
23. Financial Markets Association (FMA).
24. Securities Industry and Financial Markets Association (SIFMA).
25. www.helpforinvestors.org

<u>Summary</u>: Chapter Seven—From Charles Ponzi to Bernard Madoff: The "Ponzi" and other Investment Schemes.

1. The "Ponzi" scheme relies upon greed. It is a fraudulent investment operation that pays irrationally high returns to early investors from their own money and/or from money paid by later investors; rather than from any actual profit earned from products or services.

2. Ponzi schemes can be very enticing to the investor—particularly the early investor, but they are doomed to fail. The Ponzi system is destined to collapse because the alleged earnings, if any, are always less than the payments to investors.

Chapter Eight

The Affinity Scam

The Bernard Madoff Ponzi scheme preyed particularly heavy on Madoff's fellow Jews and Jewish organizations, destroying the fortunes and wealth of many Jewish charities and other organizations. Several of these organizations were forced to close because of Madoff's scam, and thousands of individuals were financially devastated [Peltz, Jennifer (December 26, 2008), "Madoff case brings out the bigots" (http://www.newsobserver.com)].

The Madoff Ponzi scheme is a classic example of "Affinity fraud."

Affinity fraud refers to scams that prey upon members of identifiable groups, such as racial or ethnical communities, religious groups, the elderly or professional groups, fraternal or sororital organizations, and so forth. These scams most frequently involve investments.

The fraudsters who manufacture and promote affinity scams or schemes most often are, or pretend to be, members of the affected group. They also frequently enlist prominent and respected leaders of the community or religious group to spread the word and/or endorse the scam by convincing these leaders that the scheme is worthy of investment and otherwise legitimate. All too often, these recruited leaders themselves become unknowingly and unwitting victims of the same affinity fraud. For example, in the Madoff Ponzi scheme, prominent and respected victims included, among many others, movie director Steven Spielberg and his WunderKinder Foundation, Yeshiva University, the Lappin Foundation, and the Women's Zionist Organization of America.

In sum, the affinity scam exploits the trust, friendship, and sense of camaraderie that exists in certain groups of people who have something in common—a common bond. Because of the inherent tight-knit structure of many groups—either religiously, socially, racially, nationally, or organizationally—it is frequently difficult for law enforcement officials or regulators to detect an Affinity scam.

Victims of the scheme frequently fail to inform authorities of the scam or pursue their legal remedies, preferring instead to attempt to work things out within the group or community. This is especially the case when the scammers have used respected religious leaders, or respected community leaders to convince others to join the investment scheme.

Not unusually, many affinity scams involve various pyramid schemes; where new or more recent investor money is used to make payments to earlier investors, thus, creating the false illusion that the investment is real and successful. This process lulls existing investors into believing their investment money is safe and secure, while tricking new investors into putting their money into the scheme. In the end, the victims suffer financial as well as emotional damage.

HOW TO AVOID AFFINITY FRAUD

TEN (10) POINTS

1. Regardless of how the investment scheme comes to your attention (whether by family members or other relatives, friends, colleagues, religious group members, or anyone else who inspires a bond of trust or confidence), if the scheme looks or sounds too good to be true, it probably is too good to be true.
2. Following up on 1 above, be very careful of investments which promise "guaranteed" results or incredible profits.
3. Extremely few investment opportunities are risk-free. Therefore, be very careful of any investment that claims to be without risks.
4. Promises by anyone that an investment will bring you fast and high profits, with little or no risk, are classic warnings of fraud.

5. Internet fraud is increasing rapidly. Be wary of "can't miss" investment opportunities over the Internet [see, Chapter 11, infra].

6. Legitimate investment opportunities tend to be in writing (type), and on paper (documents). Avoid so-called investment opportunities that are not documented. Word-of-mouth, alone, should be unacceptable.

7. Be very cautious of investment opportunities that are suppose to be a "secret." These so-called "secret" opportunities can frequently be harmful financially, or illegal.

8. Always investigate the investment opportunity thoroughly. Check the truth or falsity of all statements or promises made to you about the investment opportunity. Frequently, the person recommending the investment opportunity to you may end up bring a fraud victim along with you.

9. Refuse to be pressured or rushed into investing your money prior to investigating the opportunity and thinking about it thoroughly.

10. Be very skeptical of investment opportunities that are promoted as "once-in-a-lifetime," or based upon confidential or "inside" information.

[www.sec.gov/investor; www.investorwords.com; www.investopedia. com; www.nasaa.org/investor; www.sltrib.com; online.wsj.com; www.azinvestor.gov; secinvestor.wordpress.com]

<u>Summary</u>: Chapter Eight—The Affinity Scam.

1. The Bernard Madoff Ponzi case is the classic example of "Affinity fraud." Affinity fraud refers to scams that prey upon members of identifiable groups, such as racial or ethnic groups, the elderly or professional groups, fraternal or sororital groups, and so forth. In other words, the Ponzi schemer is identified as a member of the victim group.

2. Regardless of <u>how</u> the investment scheme comes to your attention (whether by family member or other relatives, friends,

colleagues, religious group members, or anyone else who inspires a bond of trust or confidence), if the scheme looks or sounds too good to be true, it probably <u>is</u> too good to be true.

3. The "Affinity" scam relies on <u>greed</u> first, and then <u>trust</u>. Always investigate the claims thoroughly before investing.

Chapter Nine

Four (4) Things Not To Do
When You Are In Debt

We as Americans are always being pushed to buy something; regardless of whether we want it . . . or need it. This fact can sometimes have humorous consequences:

> *A vacuum sales man appeared at the door of an old lady's cottage and, without allowing the woman to speak, rushed into the living room and threw a large bag of dirt all over her clean carpet. He said, "If this new vacuum doesn't pick up every bit of dirt then I'll eat all the dirt."*

> *The woman, who by this time was losing her patience, said, "Sir, if I had enough money to buy that thing, I would have paid my electricity bill before they cut it off. Now, what would you prefer, a spoon or a knife and fork?"*
> [www.debtconsolidationcare.com/forums/moneyjokes.html; by permission]

Americans spend too much money. We live in debt.

Being in Debt is not an enjoyable experience. It is simply not fun. It is, unfortunately however, a dangerous by-product of the American capitalist system.

I contend that getting out of debt is a two step process. First, the consumer must "stop the financial bleeding" by not getting further in debt. This only makes matters worse. Secondly, after "stabilizing" the patient (i.e., the debt-ridden consumer), the consumer can begin the process of eliminating the existing debt by reduced payments, negotiations, settlements, compromises, et al. Ultimately, perhaps even bankruptcy.

There are a number of methodologies and techniques touted a lot and may seem to get the consumer out of debt faster. The reality, however, is that most of these so-called "sure" debt-reduction schemes may make matters worse for the consumers in their genuine efforts to get out of debt.

For those American credit card holders, the average credit card debt amount per holder has been estimated by some authorities to be $15,788.00 [Source: aralifestyle.com (2011)].

Following are four (4) things I do <u>not</u> recommend the consumer do in an effort to get out of debt. *[Caveat: As always, it is advised that the reader or consumer contact a local and qualified professional for advice in this area]:*

1. Do not rely <u>solely</u> on "minimal payments" or small monthly payments on your credit cards to improve or even maintain your credit rating. Certainly, making minimal monthly payments, in combination with other techniques *[see, Chapter Three: Credit Bureaus, Credit Scores and the Credit Business],* may help your credit in the short term, but it will surely cost you plenty over the longer term. Your interest accumulation will far outweigh and outdistance your minimum payments.

   Making small monthly payments on your credit card debt may make you "feel better", but it prolongs your debt load . . . making more money for the credit card company.

2. Be wary or cautious about rolling your debt balance or credit card balance over to an introductory rate credit card. Again,

acquiring a low- or-no-interest rate credit card may help save some money for you in the short term as you struggle to pay the debt off; but that low interest rate can quickly, and frequently does, turn into a higher rate. This development can put you right back in the same predicament you were in previously.

3. Never assume your interest rates are constant or the same. Usually, all that the credit card companies have to do is send you a notice fifteen (15) days in advance of increasing your interest rate. This bad news is typically hidden in small print gobbledegook that no one ever reads.

   [Always remember: The **BOLD PRINT** giveth . . . and the small print taketh away [see, Chapter Ten: "Avoiding Debt Settlement Scams", number 8 of "Ten (10) Tips and Secrets for the Consumer to Avoid Debt Settlement Scams"].

4. Be wary or cautious of debt settlement scams and schemes [see, Chapter Ten, infra]. With some effort, you can usually do just as well negotiating on your own.

Many debt settlement or debt negotiation firms charge the consumer a fee to essentially work out the equivalent of minimum payments. As has been noted previously, (1, supra), making minimum payments rarely makes the debt go down. Minimum payments just pay for the new monthly interest charged each payment cycle. These payments do not go toward paying off the balance of the loan.

In fact, it has been guesstimated by at least one reliable source that it would take more than 40 years to pay off most credit cards by making just minimum payments [see, aralifestyle.com (2011)]. **[www.fool.com/personal;   articles.moneycentral.msn.com; www.consumerismcommentary.com; financialplan.about.com; thecnnfreedomproject.blogs.cnn.com].**

Predicting Household Debt Repayment Problems

Reliable economic theory states in proposition that consumers borrow money in order to level or transition their lifetime continuum of serviceability or convenient living from consumption. In other words, and in a nutshell, from time to time when families or households' income streams do not equal or match their desired current consumption or spending, they borrow against their expected future income or use previous income (savings) to finance or spend for current consumption.

This creates "consumer debt" [see, Professor Deborah D. Godwin, "Predictors Of Households' Debt Repayment Difficulties", 1989, Department of Housing and Consumer Economics, University of Georgia, Athens, Georgia 30602; published 1999, Association for Financial Counseling and Planning Education].

In a study done by Professor Deborah D. Godwin of the University of Georgia, 1,479 households in the 1983-1989 panel data of the "Survey of Consumer Finances" were examined as to the households' probability of experiencing debt repayment difficulty in 1989 [Ibid.].

The effects of "1983 household" characteristics, attitudes, and behavior regarding debt, debt portfolios, and intervening events were examined. The results showed that households more likely to experience difficulty with debt repayment during the period of 1983-1989 were:

(1) Younger;
(2) Nonwhite;
(3) Larger households (number of members);
(4) Had more positive attitudes about credit;
(5) Had previous difficulty obtaining credit;
(6) Had mortgage, automobile, or durable goods debt outstanding;
(7) Had received financial support from relatives and/or friends; and
(8) Had made major real estate transactions between 1986 and 1989.

In sum, generally, large and young households (and particularly, minority households) are more vulnerable to debt repayment problems, according to the Godwin study.

<u>Summary</u>: Chapter Nine—Four (4) Things Not To Do When You Are In Debt.

1. Do not rely solely on "minimum" or "minimal" payments or small monthly payments on your cards to improve or even maintain your credit rating. This tactic rarely works.
2. Be cautious about rolling your debt balance or credit card balance over to an introductory rate credit card. Eventually you will most likely go further in debt.
3. Never assume your interest rates are constant or the same. They can, and frequently do, increase.
4. Be wary of debt settlement scams and schemes. They rarely help.

Chapter Ten

Avoiding Debt Settlement Scams

The debt settlement industry is not immune from fraudulent schemers. If the consumer chooses to go the route of a debt settlement company, it is very important that he or she be able to recognize scams. Knowing what to do is crucial in choosing a legitimate and reputable debt settlement company.

—Charles Jerome Ware, Former Special Counsel to the Chairman of the Federal Trade Commission (FTC).

First of all, it is important for the consumer to know that "debt settlement" is <u>not</u> the same as "debt consolidation." More so than debt consolidation, debt settlement usually involves (i) unsecured debt, (ii) that generally will, to some degree, be "charged-off" (R-9 on your credit report; see Chapter Three, <u>supra</u>), and (iii) that most likely will require that the consumer be issued a 1099 from the creditor on the debt that is settled.

"Debt consolidation" programs are usually simply a large loan that pays off other smaller loans. Debt consolidation programs, too, can be beneficial to borrowers or debtors, but they also can have their failings. If the consumer is paying several different loans off, his or her life may be easier if they consolidate their debts into one loan. That way the consumer will get only one monthly statement and make only one payment each month.

Particularly during the recent economic downturn, debt settlement has become an increasingly popular tool or technique for consumers to deal with their outstanding debts. As a result, the debt settlement industry is growing fast—very fast. There are many, many companies in the market offering so-called debt settlement and/or debt negotiation services.

Certainly there are legitimate and reputable debt settlement companies in existence. Unfortunately, though, the industry is also plagued by a large number of debt settlement scams and fraudulent organizations. The best defense for the consumer in avoiding debt settlement scams is to know what to look for in choosing a legitimate and reputable company.

The following are ten (10) tips and secrets for the consumer to avoid debt settlement scams:

1. Agency contacts regarding credentials, licensing and complaints. The Federal Trade Commission (FTC) and the Better Business Bureau (BBB) may be contacted to find out if there are any consumer complaints on file or record against a particular debt settlement company. The Attorney General's Office in each state is usually able to provide the necessary information concerning licensing and credentialing of debt settlement businesses.

   It should be noted that each state has different licensing and credentialing requirements regarding for-profit debt settlement and counseling. Several states prohibit these businesses altogether. Obviously, a so-called debt settlement and/or counseling firm that attempts to solicit customers in states where they are unlicensed or prohibited is operating illegally and must be avoided.

2. Ask the company for up-to-date references. Contact at least a couple of the company's references and inquire about their experiences with the firm.

3. Research, Research, Research. Investigate the company as thoroughly as your time and resources will permit. Ask lots of questions of the company. A legitimate and reputable firm will answer them, and will not mind doing so.

4. Costs, fees and services. Following-up on 3, supra, a legitimate and reputable debt settlement company will forthrightly provide

a clear and understandable explanation of costs, fees and services to potential clients. The firm should be able to quickly and succinctly explain to the consumer precisely what it will do for him or her in exchange for the costs and fees it will be charging the consumer. This area of "costs and fees" is one of the most confusing aspects of debt settlement for the consumer.

A reputable and competent debt settlement firm should offer each consumer a precise, personalized plan of action that is specifically geared or tailored to the individual consumer's financial situation, along with a statement of what fees the company charges the consumer.

Be very cautious about debt settlement companies that require money upfront from the consumer without providing adequate specific information as outlined in 2, 3, and 4, supra, and 5, infra.

5. Alternative options and/or solutions. Sometimes, even frequently, debt settlement may not be the best choice for the consumer. If that's the case, the debt settlement company should be capable and honest enough to offer alternatives or options to the consumer. Sure, debt settlement is an option to reduce debt, but it is not always the best option. It depends on the consumer's specific factual circumstances. For example, perhaps "debt consolidation" would be a better choice for the consumer.

6. Money-back guarantee. Many legitimate and reputable debt settlement companies offer a written guarantee to the consumer. The optimal guarantee ensures consumers that if the company is unable to provide the services presented in the contract, then the firm will return the consumer's money.

Since this "money-back guarantee" is prevalent among reputable firms in the industry, the consumer naturally should request it. If the company is unwilling to accommodate the consumer in this regard, the consumer should consider the refusal as creating an unnecessary risk for him or her.

7. If what the debt settlement firm says sounds too good to be true . . . it probably is too good to be true. Generally, a good debt settlement company can be expected to save the consumer,

on average, from 40% to 60% on his or her debts. However, it takes time, money, and patience to get the best deal.

8. <u>Read the contact thoroughly</u>. Before signing-up with the selected debt settlement company, read the contract thoroughly. **Remember: the Bold (large) print in a contact, giveth, and the Fine (small) print taketh away!**

9. <u>Go online to check-up on the company</u>. Use the Internet to "google" (research) the debt settlement company. Look for consumer complaints, history, organization, <u>et al</u>.

10. <u>Due diligence</u>. Generally, engage in due diligence and do your homework when deciding whether to go the debt settlement company route and, if so, which firm to use.

Debt settlement scams are now widespread in this country, and in the world. Do your homework and follow the tips and secrets in this chapter.

[www.ehow.com; www.christiannet.com/debtsettlement; www. debtfreedestiny.com; ezinearticles.com/finance; www.bbb.org]

<u>Summary</u>: Chapter Ten—Avoiding Debt Settlement Scams

1. "Debt Settlement" is not the same as "Debt Consolidation."

2. More so than debt consolidation, debt settlement usually involves (i) unsecured debt, (ii) that generally will, to some degree, be "charged off" (R-9 on your credit report), and (iii) that most likely will require that the consumer be issued a 1099 from the creditor on the debt that is settled.

3. Be very cautious about debt settlement companies that require money upfront from the consumer without providing a precise, personalized plan of action that is specifically tailored to the individual consumer's financial situation.

4. Sometimes, even frequently, debt settlement may not be the best choice for the consumer. If that's the case, the debt settlement company should be capable, willing, and honest enough to advise the consumer accordingly and offer alternatives or options to the consumer.

5. Look for the legitimate and reputable debt settlement companies that offer a written guarantee (or "money-back guarantee") to the consumer. These companies do exist in this industry.

6. If what the debt settlement firm says sounds too good to be true, then it probably is too good to be true.

7. Generally, a good debt settlement company can be expected to save the consumer, on average, from 40% to 60% on his or her debts.

8. Before signing-up with the selected debt settlement company (or, for that matter, before any agreement in writing) read the contract carefully.

9. Remember: The Bold (large) print in a contract giveth, and the Fine (small) print taketh away!

Chapter Eleven

The "Nigerian," The "Singapore," The "Irish Lottery," and Other Internet Scams

Money stealing scams and schemes pop-up on the Internet from all nations and nationalities on a daily basis:

From: "Garry McGill"
Sent: Thursday, March 17, 2011 4:24 PM
Subject: I wait your response . . .

Dear Sir/Madam,

My Names are Mr. Thomas Gray, Staff of Nat West Bank UK. I would like you to indicate your interest to receive the transfer of $11.5 Million Dollars. I will like you to stand as the next of kin to my late client whose account is presently dormant for claims. Please once you are interested in my business proposal, further details of the transfer will be forwarded to you as soon as I receive your return mail. Click on the blow link to confirm more details behind the death of my deceased client.

Regards
Mr. Thomas Gray
Please send your Reply to my private email address.
Email:

*   *   *

From: "BELLO"
Sent: Wednesday, March 23, 2011 5:11 AM
Subject: FROM Dr Ubaka Bello

The management of UNITED TRUST BANK Nigeria Plc, after a close door meeting with CBN and IMF has concluded to pay you $2.5m as unpaid contract fund via ATM. kindly send your names, address and phone no for verification and immediate payment.

Dr Ubaka Bello
UNITED TRUST BANK Nig Plc

*   *   *

From: "Rev Fr. Paul John" <webmaster@entreyytrent.co.uk>
Sent: Wednesday, March 16, 2011 10:08 PM
Subject: ATM CARD PAYMENT NOTIFICATION
From The Desk of ReV Fr.Paul John
Director ATM Department
Intercontinental Bank Plc:

ATM CARD PAYMENT NOTIFICATION

Attn:

We the federal governing bank of the federal govt of NIGERIA reached out an aggrement with the federal executive council and the senate to use the federal reserve account to settle all out all our standing payment to all our foreign debtors.

RIGHT NOW WE HAVE ARRANGED YOUR PAYMENT OF 10.5MILLION DOLLARS THROUGH OUR SWIFT CARD

PAYMENT CENTER ASIA PACIFIC, THAT IS THE LATEST INSTRUCTION FROM THE PAYMENT PANEL I

FEDERAL REPUBLIC OF NIGERIA. THIS CARD CENTER WILL SEND YOU AN ATM CARD WHICH YOU WILL USE TO

WITHDRAW YOUR MONEY IN ANY ATM MACHINE IN ANY PART OF THE WORLD, SO IF YOU LIKE TO RECEIVE

YOUR FUND IN THIS WAY, PLEASE GET BACK TO US WITH THE REQUIRED INFORMATION BELOW.

1. FULL NAME
2. ADDRESS WERE YOU WANT US TO SEND THE ATM CARD
3. PHONE AND FAX NUMBER
4. YOUR AGE AND CURRENT OCCUPATION
5. ATTACH COPY OF YOUR IDENTIFICATION

Looking forward to serving you better.

Yours Truly
Rev Fr. Paul John
ATM Department Director
Intercontinental Nigeria Plc.

*   *   *

From: "From US Sgt Mark Humpreys" <sftmarksupri@usmil.org>
Sent: Tuesday, March 22, 2011 7:43 PM
Subject: From US Sgt. Mark Humpreys.

Hi,

How are you doing today? It's yours(Sgt.) Mark Humphreys, Tour of Duty Baghdad, US Army's 3rd Infantry Division. With a desparate call for a quick assistance, I have summed up courage to contact you found your contact particulars in an address journal am seeking for your sincere assistance to move the sum of ($18.8 Million) EIGHTEEN MILLION EIGHT HUNDRED THOUSAND DOLLARS to you, as far as I can be assured that my share of this fund will be safe in your care until I complete my tour of duty here in Baghdad.

Source of Money:

Some cash in various currencies was discovered in barrels at a farm house near Tikrit during a rescue operation, and it was agreed by staff Sgt. Kenneth Buf and I that some part of this money be shared amongst both of us before informing anybody about it since both of us saw the money first. This was quite an illegal thing to do, but I tell you what? No compensation can make up for the risk we have taken with our lives over these years and the lives of our beloved ones.

Baghdad is a hell hole; my brother in-law was killed by a road side bomb in November and his name was on the list of our latest casualties, the above figure was given to me as my share, and to conceal this kind of money while I'm still here has become a

Problem, so with the help of a British contact working here for the UNITED NATIONS VOLUNTEER DELIVERY SERVICES, his office enjoys some special ummunity around here, Iw as able to get the parcel out to a safe location entirely out of trouble spot. He

Does not know the real contents of the parcel, and he believes that it belongs to a British / American medical doctor who died in an air reaid here in Baghdad, and before giving up, trusted me to hand over the parcel to his family back home. I'll discuss this with you when I am sure that you are willing to assist me, and I believe that my money will be well secured in your hand because you have the fear of god. I want you to tell me how much you will take from this money for the assistance you will give to me.

One passionate appeal I will make to you is not to discuss this matter with anyone, should you have reasons to reject this offer, please destroy this message as any leakage of this information will be too bad for soldier's here in Iraq. Yet I don't know how long we will remain here, and I have been shot, wounded and survived two suicide attacks by the special grace of god, this and other reasons I will mention later has prompted me tor each out for help, I honestly want this matter to be resolved immediately, please contact me as soon as possible with my private e-post address which is my only source of communication.

Yours in Service,
Sgt. Mark Humphreys.

*   *   *

Scams pop-up on the Internet from all nations and all nationalities on a daily basis:

Congratulations!!! You have won
From: Irish Lottery (no.replies45@lycos.com)
Sent: Mon 2/08/10 10:16 AM
To: (Unknown)

Congratulations. Your email address has won J2,800,000.00 pounds from Irish Lottery
Draw. To claim your winning, contact Mr. Wilson on Email:

*   *   *

Barrister Olu Thomas Can Help You

From: Mrs. Debra Avalos (info@consejos-3.com)
Sent: Mon 2/08/10 6:46 AM
To: (Unknown)

Attn: My Dear,

I am Mrs. Debra Avalos, I am a US citizen, 48 years old. I reside in Buda, Texas 78610-4819. My residential address is as follows. 12107 Mustang Mesa Drive, Buda, Texas 78619-4819, United States, am thinking of relocating since I am now rich. I am one of those that took part in the Compensation in Nigeria many years ago and they refused to pay me. I had paid over $20,000USD while in the USA, trying to get my payment all to no avail. So I decided to travel down to Nigeria with all my compensation documents, and I was directed to meet Barr. Olu Thomas, who is the FOREIGN REMITTANCE AWARD COMMITTEE, and I contacted him and he explained everything to me. He said whoever is contacting us through e-mails are fake. He took me to the paying bank for the claim of my Compensation payment. Right now I am the happiest woman on earth because I have received my Compensation funds of $500,000,000 USD (Five Hundred Thousand US Dollars). Moreover, Barr. Olu Thomas showed me the full information of those that are yet to receive their payments and I saw your name and e-mail address as one of the beneficiaries that is why I decided to email you to stop dealing with those people, they are not with your fund, they are only making money out of you. I will advise you to contact Barr. Olu Thomas. You have to contact him directly with your full name, home address and phone number on this information below.

FOREIGN REMITTANCE AWARD HOUSE
Name: Barr. Olu Thomas
Email:
Phone +234-8028163825

You really have to stop dealing with those people that are contacting you and telling you that your fund is with them, it is not in anyway with them, they are only taking advantage of your and they will dry you up until you have nothing. The only money I paid after I met Mr. Kunle Martins was just $580 for the paper works, take note of that. Once again stop contacting those people, I will advise you to contact Mr. Olu Thomas so that he can help you to deliver your fund instead of dealing with those liars that will be turning you around asking for different kind of money to complete your transaction.
Thank You and Be Blessed.

Mrs. Debra Avalos
12107 Mustang Mesa Drive
Buda, Texas 78610-4819
United States

*   *   *

Can you work with me.
From: Tan Seng Chew (tansh_40@yahoo.com.sg)
Sent: Sun 2/07/10 9:49 PM
To: (Unknown)

Charles Jerome Ware

Sunday, February 07, 2010.
sengtanchew@yahoo.com.hk
Singapore.

Good day, I hope you are having a good day and this message meets you in a good mood.

I am Tan S C, and I am an employee of one of the top financial institutions here in Singapore.

I want to use this opportunity to Offer you a business undertaking with a very high monetary gain and value, mutually beneficial to both parties if you are interested.

Please allow me to give you a brief picture of what I have in mind, in November 2001 a Young Indonesian Man Named (withheld for now) opened a Foreign Currency Fixed Deposit Account (total value GBP16.9M) at my branch where I was then the Accounts manager, he was elegantly dressed and seem to be very wealthy, these are common occurrences, but what aroused my Interest what the fact the money when it finally came in was in British sterling and what we usually handled for such transactions was American dollars, so nevertheless I had an eye on the account.

Now if you have ever operated a high profile bank account or safe deposit account, you will understand that only the account officer and the teller or cashier who actually handles your deposit know who you are and all that, I was the only one aware that this deposit was made and continuously monitored the account until I found that the account holder was a fugitive wanted by governments for a lot of crimes.

I kept this information to myself because I did not want anything to happen to me or my family as the account holder had my contact details and any leak would have clearly been straight from me or so I thought.

But as faith will have it on Friday, 18 September 2009, I was elated to read that the fugitive had lost is life and the bondage that I have been under since that account was opened is now over and not only that the founds are at my disposal right now, if and only if you can pledge your concrete commitment to assist me convert this

108

funds to our personal usage immediately, all I need from you is to stand as the original depositor.

I am now currently the departmental head and I am in a very suitable position to carry out this transaction without any blow back on either of us or our families, that is why we need to act now and immediately.

Please understand I am ready to share this money with you equally for your assistance, I do know that I have not given you a clear view picture, but when I get your reply I will be more explicit.

I wait to hear form you, via my secure email below.

Your immediate response will be appreciated.

Best Regards,
Tan Seng Chew.
sengtanchew@yahoo.com.hk

*   *   *

From Madam Mendoza Cardenas
From: Mendoza Cardenas (lanphe@cantv.net)
You may not know this sender. Mark as safe | Mark as junk
Sent: Sun 2/07/10 9:12 PM
To:

_____

Dearest One,

I am madam Mendoza Cardenas, a native of Philippine nationality. I would like to have a long lasting and confident business relationship with possible entrusting my partner life time fortune into your possession. As now I am broken hearted and needs someone to trust, without remembering my past and forsaken experiences from close confidants and family. I need someone who would take me for whom I am and as a life partner.

antoaphrase-

Well, from your profile I believe in me that you ought to be honest person. I would like to give you a brief description of my life. I am the Secretary of senator Antonio Fuentes Trillanes, who was arrested and since detained by the government forces on the 29th day of November 2007.

You may wish to update yourself with more information of my Boss' official pictures and news about my partner here: (http://www.worldpress.org/Asia/3007.cfm).

But not quite long, I was also arrested along with my Boss, not been released. All I want from you is to assist me make claim funds, he did deposited in China, the Amount being deposited is much about 10 million USD.

All I want from you is honesty and sincerity, as soon as this money claimed by you, I will advise you on how to wire some money to me to enable me pay off the chief justice for his demand in getting my partner out of prison. And then fly over to meet you. I wait your reply for more details.

Sincerely yours,
Madam Mendoza Cardenas

———————————————

Subject: Attention: E-mail Address Owner

Attention: E-mail Address Owner

RE: 2011ok SCAM VICTIM'S COMPENSATION FROM THE Ministry of Finance Benin Republic, The Ministry of Finance is compensating all the scam victims and your email address was found in the scam victim's list. This Western Union office has been mandated by the Ministry of Finance to transfer your compensation to you via West Union Money Transfer.

However, we have concluded to affect your own payment through Western Union Money Transfer, $5,000 twice daily

110

until the total sum of $1,500.00 is completely transferred to you. We can not be able to send the payment with your email address alone, thereby we need your information as to where we will be sending the funds such as;

Receiver's name: . . . .

Address: . . . .

Country: . . . .

Phone number: . . . .

Also western union demanded that we must pay for the remittance of the check before the release of the pick up information of first $5000USD to you. And this is $98USD which has to be paid through Samuel James O. at Western Union Office.

Contact our Customer Care at (western.union38@w.cn) with your full information.

Note that your payment files will be returned to the Ministry Of Finance within 24 hours if we did not hear from you, this was the instruction given to us by the Ministry of Finance.

We will start the transfer as soon as we have received your information and confirmed from the western union that you have paid the remittance of the check. For urgent inquiry email and call this phone number +229)98095084; western. union38@w.cn

Thanks,
Mr. Daniel Kevin.
The agent incharge.

CONFIDENTIAL NOTICE
This email is intended for the owner of this E-mail Address only and contains privileged and confidential information. If you received this email by error, please delete it from your mail box and notify us immediately for correction. The disclosure of this email to a third party is highly prohibited. Thanks for your understanding.

Subject: RE:NOTIFICATION FOR YOUR ATM MASTER CARD.

Attn: Beneficiary,

We hereby officially notifying you about the present arrangement to pay you, your over due contract/inheritance fund through (ATM CARD) This arrangement was initiated/constituted by the World Bank, Paris club and central bank of Ghana, due to impostors activities going on around the world, We Hereby Issued You Our Code Of Conduct, Which Is (ATM-202).

The World Bank and Paris Club introduced this payment arrangement as to enable our contractors/inheritance beneficiary to receive their fund without any interference. The ATM CARD are powered by GOLD CARD WORLD WIDE.

Upon the receipt of this mail your fund is going to be load into the ATM CARD and a scan copy of the card will be send to you before we will proceed to dispatch the card directly to your nominated home address so you absolutely have nothing to worry about all we need is your Prompt Response and Co-operation by Gods Grace we will have a successful Transaction.

In View of this,you are advised to contact the Director (OBB,IRD,ATM) Dr Robert Smith for further information with the following contact below as soon as you receive this message for further update. Please call the ATM Company immediately you receive this message for better explanation.

Contact Person: Dr.Robert Smith
Tel: +233 547 599 947
Emails: (atmpaymentoffice@list.ru)

Reconfirm the following information to him for Security reason.

1. Full Name: . . . .
2. Phone and Fax Number: . . . .
3. Address Were You Want Them To Send The ATM Card To (P.O Box Not Acceptable): . . . .
4. Your Age And Current Occupation: . . . .
5. Attach Copy Of Your Identification: . . . .
6. Email: . . . .

Best regards,
Mr Nguru Jeffrey,
Financial Secretary.
Foreign Operation Department.

Subject: CONTACT DR EZE OVILIVO JOHN FOR YOUR PAYMENT

Urgent Attention,

The Board of federal ministry of finance benin republic. Are here to notify you of your payment inheritance funds of $4,400.000.00 UNITED STATES,after the meeting held on 26/02 2011. His Exelence the PRESIDENT OF FEDERAL REPUBLIC OF BENIN DR YAYi BONI.has Instructed this Department to pay all the people who lost their fund through scam in this country and your among of them he said we should pay them and your are on of those people so we will send your funds through western union money transfer every day payment or for easier wire transfer for quick receive of your inherinted funds without any further delay.

To avoid paying money to the fraud stars that is going on through the global,You are required to send your name and address or bank info were you want your fund to be sending through western union the maximum amount you will be receiving every day starting from

113

today is the sum of $6500.00.also your are required to send us the sum of $167.00 for Re-newing and econfirming your payment file.

Beneficiarey name---------------------------------
Address-----------------------------
Tel phone----------------------------
your age-----------------------------
your occupation-----------------------------
your bank info if you want it by wire transfer-------------------------

CONTACTPERSON,DR   EZEOVILIVO   JOHN,EMAIL: ministryfinace@hosanna.net)   ministry_ng@sify.com   Tele +229-974-988-76 As soon required fee of $167.00 and your full info was send today for the renewing and reconfirming your payment file you will start receiving your funds as from tomorrow,Send the $167.00 dollar through western union Amount—$167.00 If your ready to send the money get back to this office to give you receivers name and wher you can send the $167.00 We are awaiting to receive the western union payment informations today,

Yours in service
Mr Samuel ckeke

Subject: GOD IS GOOD

I am Kristen Lynne Boyd, a British & Northern Ireland Citizen by Nationality. I'm 77 years old woman without a child to inherit my fortunes due to UTERINE FIBROID TUMORS CANCER which denied my pregnancy. I have undergone several medical treatments of UTERINE FIBROID TUMORS CANCER in other to be pregnant but all efforts were in vain. I inherited my late father assets and funds, few weeks ago my doctor revealed to me that due to my UTERINE FIBROID TUMORS CANCER, I have number of weeks to live here on earth.

Though I have made several donations out of most of my properties to relatives and my well wishers around but as much pressure mounted on my healths, I can figure out what will happen next to me, Therefore, I decided to contact you, to solicit your support and assistance to kindly assist me with the distributions of these funds to Churches, Schools, Charity Homes, Less Privileges and Public Hospital in your State. The amount is UKGBP 11,450,000,000.00 Million British pounds is still with the Security Company in London and below is how the funds are going to be use, If you are willing and have interest to assist me on this please get in touch with me by email me for more details.

1) UKGBP 3,450,000,000 Three Million four hundred fifty thousand British pounds should be for you and your family members:
2) UKGCP 2,000,000.000 Two Million British pounds should be shared to the public hospital in your State:
3) UKGBP 3,000,000,000 Four Million British pounds should be shared to the charity homes and less privilege in your State:
4) UKGBP 3,000,000,000 Two Million British pounds be sharing to churches, schools in your State:

I look forward to hearing from you.
Kristen Lynne Boyd.

ANALYSIS

All of these Internet scams have fundamental elements in common:

1. They have catchy and/or intriguing topics and headlines:

    — "GOD IS GOOD"
    — "Congratulations!!! You have won!"
    — "Barrister Olu Thomas Can Help You."

— "Can you work with me."
— "From Madam Mendoza Cardenas."
— "Contact Dr. E.O. John for your payment".
— "Respond immediately . . . . !!!"
— "Hello."
— "United Nations Assisted Program (UNAP)
    Debit Reconciliation Department
    Direct of International Payment."

2. They frequently, though not always, either make reference to, or originate from, foreign countries:

— Africa.
— "Irish Lottery" (Ireland).
— Nigeria.
— Singapore.
— Philippines, China.
— Federal Republic of Benin.

3. They are all mass-produced and mass-distributed to potential consumer victims:

— "To: (Unknown)."
— "To: (Unknown)."
— "To: (Unknown)."
— "To: Undisclosed Recipients."
— "To: Unpaid Beneficiary."

4. They all promise an exorbitant amount of money, amounting to unrealistic expectations on the part of the consumer victims *(Remember: If the scheme looks or sounds too good to be true, it usually is too good to be true):*

— "J2,800,000.00 pounds."
— "$500,000.000 USD."
— "high monetary gain and value . . . GBP16.9M."

— "10 million USD."

— "UKGBP 11,450,000,000.00 Million British pounds"

— "The amount is UKGBP 11,450,000,000.00 Million British pounds is still with the Security Company in London and below is how the funds are going to be use, If you are willing and have interest to assist me on this please get in touch with me by email me for more details."

1) UKGBP 3,450,000,000 Three Million four hundred fifty thousand British pounds should be for you and your family members:

2) UKGCP 2,000,000.000 Two Million British pounds should be shared to the public hospital in your State:

3) UKGBP 3,000,000,000 Four Million British pounds should be shared to the charity homes and less privilege in your State:

4) UKGBP 3,000,000,000 Two Million British pounds be sharing to churches, schools in your State:"

— "This email is to notify you about the release of your outstanding payment which is truly $10 million (TEN MILLION UNITED STATES DOLLARS) . . . ."

— ". . . You have been selected for a cash Price of? 450,000.00 (four hundred and fifty thousand Great British Pounds) and a brand-new BMW 2010 M5 Sedan Car from International programs held . . . in the United Kingdom . . . "

— ". . . your share will be 40% . . . ."

5. Allegedly, in order to acquire the unrealistically high sum of money, the consumer must send (usually via wire) money to the scammers:

— ". . . Contact Mr. Wilson (who will give the consumer instructions via email how they will separate the consumer from his or her money) . . . ."

— ". . . just $480 . . . ."

117

— "I wait to hear from you, via my secure email below (and I will separate you gladly from your hard-earned money)."
— "I will advise you on how to wire some money to me . . . ."
— "Also Western Union demanded . . ."

6. There is usually a third-party who will ultimately receive your money to make the deal operate (but occasionally there are exceptions):

— ". . . Contact Mr. Wilson . . . ."
— "(contact) Barrister Olu Thomas directly."
— ". . . I do know that I have not given you a clear view picture (of how I am going to steal your money from you), but when I get your reply I will be more explicit."
— ". . . I will advise you on how to wire some money to me to enable me (to) pay off the chief justice for his demand in getting my partner out of prison."
— "You are advised to contact the Director (OBB, JRD, ATM) Dr. Robert Smith for further information . . ."

7. The writing is usually relatively elementary, or verbosely overdone with excessive illiterate flourish; and is frequently unintelligible:

— ". . . I hope you have a good day and this message meets you in good mood."
— ". . . Now if you have ever operated a high profile bank account or safe deposit account, you will understand that only the account officer and the teller or cashier who actually handles your deposit know who you are and all that, I was the only one aware that this deposit was made and continuously monitored the account until I found that the account holder was a fugitive wanted by governments for a lot of crimes."
— ". . . But as faith will have it on Friday, 18 September 2009, I was elated to read that the fugitive had lost is life and

the bondage that I have been under since that account was opened is now over and not only that the founds are at my disposal right now, if and only if you can pledge your concrete commitment to assist me convert this funds to our personal usage immediately, all I need from you is to stand as the original depositor."

— "to avoid paying money to the fraud stars that is going on through the global,You are required to send your name and address or bank info were you want your fund to be sending through western union the maximum amount you will be receiving every day starting from today is the sum of $6500.00.also your are required to send us the sum of $167.00 dollar for Re-newing and econfirming your payment file."

— "In View of this,you are advised to contact the Director (OBB,IRD,ATM) Dr Robert Smith for further information with the following contact below as soon as you receive this message for further update. Please call the ATM Company immediately you receive this message for better explanation."

— "Though I have made several donations out of most of my properties to relatives and my well wishers around but as much pressure mounted on my healths, I can figure out what will happen next to me, Therefore, I decided to contact you, to solicit your support and assistance to kindly assist me with the distributions of these funds to Churches, Schools, Charity Homes, Less Privileges and Public Hospital in your State."

Avoid these Internet scams.

[www.idtheftcenter.org (ITRC, 2011); www.fbi.gov/scams (FBI, 2011); www.ftc.gov (FTC, 2011)]

Everyone is a potential target of scammers.

Internet scammers frequently do not discriminate among their victims. Even the so-called more well-heeled and sophisticated individuals and organizations in our society are targets of scammers. Greed is no respecter of social status, education, wealth or sophistication. As an example, check out the 2011 case of the "Nigerian" scam pulled on hundreds of lawyers in the U.S. and Canada:

A "Nigerian" Scam Snatches Over $31,000,000.00 Out of Lawyers

In August 2011, it became public that the country of Nigeria had extradited to the United States a man who was then indicted for allegedly scamming more than $31 million out of more than 80 law firms in the U.S. and Canada [Associated Press (AP) and ABA Journal News, August 19, 2011].

The scam appears to have worked as follows: One of several scammers would contact (usually by way of the Internet) a lawyer or law firm allegedly for legal assistance in collecting a debt. He becomes the client. Another scammer acting as the debtor would send a fake check to the law firm or lawyer, who would deposit the check into its escrow account and take out the firm's fee before sending the balance to the alleged client. On the occasion when this "Nigerian" scam was carried out successfully, the alleged client got the money before the fake check was discovered.

It is hard to believe this scam would work on lawyers, but apparently it did. The indictment of this individual alleges that this "Nigerian" fraud group collected more than $31 million in this scam and tried without success to defraud an additional $100 million out of another 300 or more lawyers.

Summary: Chapter Eleven. The "Nigerian," The "Singapore," The "Irish Lottery," and Other Internet Scams

1. Scams pop-up on the Internet from all nations and nationalities on a daily basis. They rely on consumer greed for their success.

2. These types of Internet offerings usually promise an exorbitant amount of money, amounting to unrealistic expectations on the part of the consumer victims.
3. If the Internet offering looks or sounds too good to be true, it usually is too good to be true. Avoid greed.
4. Everyone is a potential target of scammers.

Chapter Twelve

Home Improvement Consumer Secrets and Tips

Generally, there is a developing consensus that the average consumer should be cautious about doing business with any company that pursues him or her "too aggressively."

What does "too aggressively" mean? Consumer groups define this action in examples as follows: numerous unsolicited flyers on your door, unsolicited mailings of advertisements, unsolicited telephone calls, door-to-door solicitations, et al., usually for such products and services as home remodeling, house painting, carpet cleaning, deck building, and other work. It is strongly recommended that you conduct your own research on the firms and hire the professional of your choice.

A. <u>Home Improvement: Secrets, Tips, Problems and Scams</u>. Home improvement is a key ingredient of home ownership. If you are not satisfied with the work done by a home improvement contactor, you have certain rights in most states [www.attorneygeneral.gov (2011); www.dllr.state.md/mhic (2011); www.ftc.gov/bcp (2011)].

<u>Licensed Home Improvement Contractor</u>

1. First of all, be sure to hire a licensed home improvement contractor. That way, if the consumer is not satisfied with the work done (or not done) by the contractor, he or she can

report it (file a complaint) with their state home improvement commission or board, or other licensing agency, and seek reimbursement from the state's guaranty fund.

The Maryland Home Improvement Commission (MHIC)

For example, the Maryland Home Improvement Commission (MHIC) licenses and regulates home improvement contractors, subcontractors and sales persons. Home improvement work (as defined in Maryland) includes alteration, remodeling, repair or replacement of a building or part of a building used as a residence. Home improvement (as defined in Maryland) also includes work done on individual condominium units. It does not include work done on commonly owned areas of condominiums or buildings that contain four or more single family units.

The MHIC investigates complaints by homeowners, awards monetary damages against licensed contractors, and prosecutes violators of the home improvement law and regulations [www.dllr. state.md/mhic (2011)].

MHIC Guaranty Fund

The MHIC, like several other states, has a Guaranty Fund (the Fund) established by assessments to licensed contractors. This Fund compensates homeowners for actual monetary losses due to poor workmanship or failure to perform a home improvement contract. The Fund applies only to work done by licensed contractors. Each licensed contractor is covered by the fund for up to $100,000 for all claims. However, the amount which can be awarded per homeowner is $20,000. The applicant contractor who submits a surety bond to meet the Commission's financial solvency requirements must submit a $20,000 bond.

What happens when the Consumer has a Complaint against an Unlicensed Home Improvement Contractor?

Good question! Essentially the consumer has about two (2) options for relief: (i) a civil action in just about all states, and (ii) in some states, a criminal action.

(i) The <u>civil action</u> would be a civil complaint in the appropriate state court or the appropriate state administrative agency filed by the consumer against the unlicensed home improvement contractor for damages and/or restitution for the alleged harm done.

(ii) In some states such as Maryland, the consumer could file the equivalent of a criminal action (subjecting the unlicensed home improvement contractor to restitution, damages, fines and penalties up to and including jail or incarceration). If the defendant unlicensed contractor fails to pay the plaintiff consumer pursuant to court order, the contractor can be jailed: the equivalent of **debtors' prison.**

U.S. Federal Trade Commission (FTC)

2. The Consumer Protection Bureau of the Federal Trade Commission has compiled an excellent list of important facts for the consumer to know before he or she hires a home improvement contractor [www.ftc.gov/bcp (2011)].

The State Attorney General

3. Many state attorneys general, including the Maryland Attorney General, offer excellent tips on home improvement contractor scams.

The Better Business Bureau (BBB)

4. The Better Business Bureau (BBB) is a national non-profit organization organized to solve business problems through the use of voluntary self-regulation and consumer education. The consumer can file a complaint against a business, as well

as search for consumer tips on the BBB website [www.bbb.org/US/homeimprovement (2011)].

5. What to do if or when you are not satisfied with the work done by a home improvement contractor:

    (a) First, contact the contractor in writing with your concerns. Give them a reasonable chance to correct the problem.

    (b) Secondly, if the contractor does not correct the problem within a reasonable period of time, file a complaint against (if licensed) your state's home improvement commission, board, or agency. In Maryland, that agency is the Maryland Home Improvement Commission (MHIC), 410 230 6309.

    (c) The consumer could also have the work completed by some other licensed home improvement contractor, and sue (even if the original contractor is unlicensed).

B. Ten (10) Tips on Hiring and Working with a Home Improvement Contractor:

1. Look for Experience. Look for a licensed home improvement contractor who has direct experience in the type of work project you have in mind. Talk to at least two experienced and licensed contractors.

2. Ask for References from satisfied customers or other professionals in related building trades.

3. Check for Customer Complaints against the licensed contractor with the state home improvement agency and the Better Business Bureau (BBB).

4. Do not be offended as a consumer if the contractor inquires about your creditworthiness and ability to pay.

5. Determine in advance what fees you, as the consumer, are expected to pay, such as:

    — a percentage surcharge above actual costs for materials;

— a small fee for a credit check;

— interest or finance charges if payments are not received as promised; and

— attorney's fees and collection costs if full payments are not received.

6. <u>Decide with the contractor in advance how disputes will be resolved</u>. For example, arbitration, mediation, court, etc.

7. <u>Always make sure changes to the contract are in writing</u>.

8. <u>Seriously consider hiring an attorney to review your contract with the contractor</u>, particularly when the amount of money involved is over $5,000 or so.

9. <u>Read the contract very carefully before signing</u>, and make sure you understand it.

10. And remember when reading the contract: *The Bold (large) print giveth, and the Fine (small) print taketh away.*

<u>Summary</u>: Chapter Twelve—Home Improvement Consumer Secrets and Tips

1. The average consumer should be very cautious about doing business with any company that pursues him or her "too aggressively." Home improvement schemers are known for their aggressiveness; including door-to-door fliers, street corner signs, "cold" calling, etc.

2. Be sure to hire a licensed home improvement contractor.

3. Many states have a Guaranty Fund (the Fund) for consumer victims that is established by assessments to licensed contractors. The Fund compensates homeowners for actual monetary losses due to poor workmanship or failure to perform a home improvement contract by a licensed home improvement contractor.

4. Always make sure changes to your home improvement contract are in writing.

5. **Debtors' Prison Warning for Unlicensed Home Improvement Contractors.**

If you are an <u>un</u>licensed home improvement contractor in the state of Maryland (and several other states as well), you could end up in "debtors' prison". Here's how:

Say, for example, in Maryland you as an unlicensed home improvement contractor performed work for a consumer and it did not go well for you nor the consumer. The dissatisfied consumer could file criminal charges against you for restitution and damages allegedly caused by you. With the criminal conviction and jail time hanging over your head, you as the unlicensed contractor could be required to pay the court-order restitution and damages to the consumer. Should you not pay these court-ordered monies to the consumer in a timely manner, you could be jailed for contempt of court or violation of the court's order.

It happens more than you can imagine.

Chapter Thirteen

Dark Secrets of Credit Cards
and Debit Cards

Credit cards and debit cards can be dangerous to the consumer's financial health. Very dangerous.

Both credit cards and debit cards are types of "electronic money" that the consumer can use to pay bills instead of using cash. Each card—credit or debit—is different; requiring different procedures to be followed when they are lawfully used, and when each card is used without the consumer's permission.

A **debit card** (also called a check card) consolidates the functions of an ATM card and a check. A **credit card** is essentially an expensive short term loan in which the consumer can "charge" items up to his or her "credit limit" (that is, the maximum amount of the loan). Both cards encourage the consumer to spend more than he or she normally would spend.

The consumer can use a **debit card** both to access cash from an ATM machine or to pay for items at a retailer. With a **debit card**, the money the consumer spends is automatically deducted from his or her bank account, therefore there are no loans or interest charges involved.

When a **credit card** bill comes, the consumer pays the amount of the short term loan back. Should the consumer be unable to pay the **credit card** bill in full each time it arrives and becomes due, the consumer will be required to pay interest to the credit card company. Many credit card companies also charge "annual fees" to the consumer, and usually will also charge additional and/or different rates for cash advances.

Banks and credit card companies make billions of dollars off consumers and the credit and debit cards [www.nytimes.com (2009); www.direct.gov (2011)].

A. Consumer Use of Debit Cards and Credit Cards

Banks prefer that the consumer uses debit cards over credit cards.

In fact, resulting from a well-planned and aggressive marketing scheme by the banks over the past decade or so, debit cards are now preferred over credit cards by American consumers. Consumer spending with debit cards, as recently as 2009, accounted for about 60 percent of retail purchases in the United States [The Nilson Report]. Debit cards are particularly popular among the group card issuers called "Generation P," for plastic. This group is composed of women, primarily, and other consumers between ages 18 and 25 [The Federal Reserve, a study].

Card issuers have money-making (for them) reasons or motives for encouraging consumers to get and use their debit card more often:

1. Card issuers make more money from the consumer who uses debit cards rather than no-fee credit cards (or better yet, cash), in the scenario in which the consumer pays off his or her card balance each month because the credit card allows the consumer to keep his or her cash longer in an interest-bearing account until the card bill is due.

2. Further, the credit card provides the consumer more leverage if he or she gets into a dispute with a merchant or retailer over some issue involving the merchandise. The consumer has much less leverage using the debit card. Once the sales transaction is done, both the retailer and the card issuer have immediately made their money.

3. Similarly to 2, above, when the consumer uses his or her debit card to authorize a transaction by entering their

personal identification number (PIN), their bank account is immediately debited the amount of the transaction plus fees and costs. On the other hand, if the consumer chooses instead to authorize payment by signing a sales slip, as he or she normally would do with a credit card, the payment is processed through a credit card network and the actual withdrawal of money from the consumer's bank account occurs later (usually within a couple days or so).

4. Regardless of which card the consumer uses—debit or credit, the banks make a lot of money when they are used.

5. Retailers generally prefer that the consumer uses PIN transactions because they (the retailers) get paid faster and are better protected with subsequent disputes with the consumer.

6. Banks, on the other hand, generally like to encourage consumers to sign the sales slip for purchases, and encourage the consumer to do so by offering mileage points or other "rewards" incentives for signature-based debit or credit payments.

7. In truth, signature transactions with cards are most profitable for banks than PIN transactions, since the interchange fees that banks get from merchants for processing signature payments is much higher than for PIN transactions.

   For example, on a $100 purchase, the bank that issued the card to the consumer typically collects about 20 cents or more in interchange fees when payment is made using a PIN. However, the same transaction using the consumer's signature yields at least seven times more (or, at least $1.40) for the bank [Litan, Avivah, Sr. Analyst, Gartner, Stamford Ct.; www.consumerreports.org].

8. Since bank marketing research shows that consumers who use **debit cards** are more often likely to <u>overdraw</u> their checking accounts, card-issuing banks make millions of dollars every year from "nonsufficient-funds fees" [Mercator Advisory Group, Waltham, Mass.; www.consumerreports. org].

9. Since 2003, banks have made billions of dollars from consumers' use of **debit cards** for purchases and ATM transactions that have exceeded the debit card holders' bank balances. In fact, the number of banks using overdraft software packages has increased by over 80 percent since 2003. [Check New Federal Law on this, effective 2010]

10. This overdraft software package traditionally allows banks to pay overdrafts of consumers <u>without</u> alerting consumers that they are exceeding their balances. These consumers (bank customers) generally do not realize that the bank is charging them a hefty fee, averaging over $30 per overdraft. This high overdraft fee is essentially a finance charge for a short-term overdraft loan, which the bank quickly snatches from the consumer account holder's next bank deposit [Center for Responsible Lending, a consumer advocacy group]. Federal Law, in 2010, has changed this scenario.

11. Racking up overdraft fees (10, <u>supra</u>) can quickly cause the consumer's **debit card** to become the most expensive credit card on the market.

12. Of the estimated $17.5 billion in overdraft loan fees that consumers pay to banks annually in the United States, nearly half are caused by **debit cards** transactions and ATM withdrawals.

13. A process or practice called "blocking" can also increase overdrafts for the **debit card** holder. Many hotels, service stations, rental car companies, and other retailers will put a "hold" on a consumer's bank funds in their checking account until a **debit card** transaction is processed. This can take several days in many instances for signature-based payments, causing an overdraft in the consumer's account.

14. This issue (13, <u>supra</u>) is compounded by the fact that the amount blocked by the retailer frequently exceeds significantly the actual amount of the consumer's purchase. For example, when the consumer swipes his or her **debit card** for $20 worth of gasoline, $280 of your bank account balance may be temporarily "blocked" because the system

is unaware of whether the consumer is filling up a small or a large car until the transaction is completely settled. If the consumer is running a low account balance, "blocking" can lead to multiple overdrafts and high fees.

15. Therefore, because of 14, <u>supra</u>, debit cards are not a good idea for large purchases such as car rentals and hotels, where hundreds of dollars may be tied up in the consumer's bank account.

[It is advised, in order to avoid costly overdraft fees, that the consumer (i) record all debit transactions in his or her check register, (ii) regularly monitor his or her account balance online, and (iii) sign-up for overdraft protection linked to a savings account].

16. Pursuant to Federal law, the consumer's liability for fraudulent charges on a **debit card** can be <u>greater</u> than the liability for a credit card. With a **debit card**, the consumer can lose up to $500 if he or she does not report the theft or loss or a card of PIN within 2 business days of discovering the problem. With a credit card, the consumer is only responsible for up to $50 in unauthorized purchases.

17. It gets worse, in 16, <u>supra</u>. If the consumer fails to report the unauthorized charges within 60 days of the date of the statement that lists them, the consumer could be held liable for <u>any</u> unauthorized withdrawals after that date.

B. <u>Three Steps To Avoid Debit-Card "Skimming" Scams</u>

1. <u>Do not type on or use your PIN at the gas pump</u>. Use your credit card rather than your debit card when purchasing gas (or, of course, use cash). There are only a couple of manufacturers of gasoline pumps in use in the United States. It is relatively easy for thieves to acquire and insert skimming devices in the pump to acquire the consumer's debit card information.

If, for some reason, you must use a debit card at the gas pump, choose the screen prompt that identifies your card as a credit card so that you are not required to type in your PIN on the machine.

2. Use only the ATM located at banks. In order to reduce the consumer's risk of loss at ATMs, he or she should use the ATMs at banks instead of the ones at convenience stores, service stations, airports, or any other isolated location [U.S. Secret Service; Darrin Blackford]. It is easier for thieves to attach and retrieve skimming devices in non-bank settings where there is less traffic and minimal surveillance cameras.

3. Carefully monitor your bank accounts. Check your bank account statements on a regular basis; preferably online rather than waiting for monthly statements to arrive in the mail. This increases your chances of finding irregularities.

C. **30 Credit Card and Debit Card Fraud Prevention Secrets and Tips**

1. When dealing with and using credit cards and debit cards, always use common sense.

2. Never carry more credit or debit cards with you than you plan to use.

3. Never reveal your Social Security number, mother's maiden name, pet's name, favorite color, or account number to strangers who contact you; particularly by telephone, the Internet, or by mail.

4. Never provide your credit card or debit card information on a website that is not secure.

5. Never write your PIN on your credit or debit card, or even have your PIN anywhere near your credit or debit card (especially in the event that your wallet or purse is stolen).

6. Never respond to emails that ask you to provide your credit card information, and never respond to emails that request you to go to a website to verify personal (and credit or debit card) information.

These are called "phishing" scams (see, Chapter Five, <u>supra</u>, "Avoiding Identity Theft and Identity Fraud").

7. Always keep an eye on your credit card and debit card every time you use it. Always make sure you get it back as quickly as possible. When taking it out of your purse or wallet, always keep it in your sight.

8. Always be extremely careful to whom you give your debit or credit card. Never give out your card's account number over the telephone unless <u>you</u> specifically initiate the call and know absolutely that the company is reputable and trustworthy.

9. Never give your credit or debit card information out when you <u>receive</u> a telephone call. Legitimate companies do not call you to ask for a credit card or debit card number over the telephone.

10. Sign (execute) your credit cards or debit cards as soon as you receive them in the mail.

11. Shred all credit card applications you receive in the mail.

12. Never leave your credit or debit cards lying around anyplace (even your bedroom).

13. Always shield or cover your credit card or debit card number so that others around you cannot see or copy it, or photograph it on a camera or cell phone.

14. Always keep a list in a secure, safe place with all of your credit card and debit card numbers and expiration dates; as well as the telephone numbers and addresses of each bank that has issued you a debit or credit card. Keep this list updated each time you receive a new credit or card.

15. We recommend a home safe, or similar secure (and fireproof) container for these and other valuable items (see 14, above).

16. Open and review credit card and debit card statements immediately upon receipt, and check to make sure the charges and accounts are accurate.

17. Treat your credit card and debit card statements the same as you should do your bank account (checking and savings). Reconcile them frequently.

18. Save all of your credit card and debit card receipts for at least 3 years (see, Chapter Five, supra). Compare them with your monthly bills and bank statements.

19. If you find any charges that you do not have a receipt for, or do not recognize, report these charges immediately in writing to the credit card or debit card issuer.

20. Always void and destroy incorrect receipts.

21. Unless you are saving them for a specific and important purpose, shred anything with your credit card or debit card number written on it.

22. Never sign (execute) a blank credit card receipt.

23. Always draw a line through the blank portions of the receipt where additional charges could be fraudulently or falsely added.

24. Destroy any and all carbon paper that is used in a credit card transaction. These days this occasion should be rare, since carbon paper is rarely used now.

25. Never write your credit card account number or debit card number in a public place, such as on a post card or so that the number shows through the envelope payment window.

26. This may be impractical but, ideally, it is generally best that you carry your debit cards and credit cards separately from your wallet. Perhaps you can carry them in a zippered compartment or a small, secure pouch.

27. Never lend a credit or debit card to anyone.

28. If you move your home, or other identified location, notify your credit and debit card issuers prior to your change of address.

29. If your credit cards or debit cards are lost, stolen, or misplaced for a concerning period of time, contact the card issuers immediately.

30. If you suspect credit card or debit card fraud, contact the card issuers immediately.

Debit Card Fraud—The Electronic Fund Transfer Act (EFTA)

The Electronic Fund Transfer Act (EFTA; 15USC 1693, et seq) of 1978 is the principal Federal law which outlines procedures involving fraud of the type that occurs when using debit cards. The law, among other things, limits the amount of money the consumer is responsible for on charges made to his or credit card without their permission [www.ftc.gov/bcp; www.fdic.gov].

The EFTA of 1978 requires all financial institutions to follow specific error resolution procedures when notified by a consumer about an alleged error involving their asset account and an electronic—funds—transfer (EFT). Conceptually, the Act is intended to protect consumers who engage in electronic fund transfers. In order for an EFT to be under the jurisdiction of the EFTA of 1978, it must (i) involve a transfer of funds, (ii) be initiated by electronic means, and (iii) either credit or debit a consumer's account. The Act specifically includes ATM transactions in its definition of EFTs [www.krcl.net; www.fdic.gov; www.eftacourt.com; www.docmagie.com].

Among other things, the EFTA requires that an ATM operator disclose the fee that a consumer is charged for an ATM transaction by providing free notices on the exterior of the ATM and the ATM screen. A failure by the ATM operator to comply with the EFTA may result in significant liability, including, among other things, liability to the consumer in an amount equal to the sum of (1) any actual financial damages suffered by the consumer; (2) statutory damages; and (3) attorneys' fees and costs.

Actual damages include the fees that a consumer was charged in the absence of proper notice.

Statutory damages are determined by the court based on (i) the frequency and persistence of noncompliance, (ii) the nature of noncompliance, (iii) the extent to which the noncompliance was intentional, (iv) the resources of the defendant, and (v) the number of persons adversely affected.

Credit Card Fraud—The Fair Credit Billing Act (FCBA)

The Fair Credit Billing Act is the primary Federal law that outlines procedures that both the consumer and the credit card company must follow when dealing with possible cases of fraud [www.ftc.gov/bcp/os/statutes/fcb; www.fdic.gov; www.creditorweb. com/definition/faircreditbillingact].

The Act provides a process for the consumer to dispute several scenarios that typically appear on the consumer's account statements. These scenarios may include, for instance, (i) charges that appear for goods and/or services the consumer never received, (ii) goods that were damaged at the time of receipt by the consumer, (iii) errors that appear in the amount the consumer should have been charged or (iv) the date the charges should be been posted, (v) credits the consumer is entitled to but have not yet shown up on his or her statement, (vi) consumer account statements mailed by the credit card company to incorrect addresses (provided, of course, the consumer properly notified the credit card issuer within the time period outlined in the Act), and (vii) the consumer's right to question any charge appearing on his or her statement that the consumer does not recognize [The Fair Credit Billing Act (FCBA); www.credtorweb.com].

When the consumer engages in these actions, the credit card company must collect documentation and things related to the charge and/or the statement and present the information to the consumer. Should the credit card company fail to take these responsive steps, the consumer will not be responsible for paying the credit card company the amount at issue.

Summary: Chapter Thirteen. Dark Secrets of Credit Cards and Debit Cards

1. Debit cards and credit cards can be dangerous to the consumer's financial health; particularly since they are types of "electronic money" with high fees and risks associated with their use.

"Electronic money" is dangerous because, for the most part, it is invisible money.

2. Generally, banks make more money from the consumers' use of debit cards over credit cards.

3. Debit cards are particularly popular among the group banks and other card issuers called "Generation P," for plastic. This group is composed of women and other consumers between ages 18 and 25.

4. Of the estimated $17.5 billion in overdraft fees that consumers pay to banks annually in the United States, nearly half are caused by debit card transactions and ATM withdrawals.

5. If the consumer must use a card for a purchase, a credit card is preferable to a debit card.

Chapter Fourteen

Franchising—Opportunities and Scams

"Franchise:" A special privilege granted to an individual or group willing to invest a specified sum of money in order to obtain the right to market products or services under the name of the corporation selling the franchise. [Investor Alert!, 1998, The Counsel for Better Business Bureaus and The North American Securities Administrators Association]

One of the areas of law and business that the Federal Trade Commission (FTC) is best known for is its promulgation and enforcement of the "Franchise Rule," which was originally enacted by the FTC in 1978.

The Federal Trade Commissions Franchise Rule gives prospective purchasers of franchises the material information these franchise consumers need in order to weigh the risks and benefits of such an investment. The Rule requires franchisors (sellers of the franchises) to provide all potential franchisees (purchasers of the franchises) with a disclosure document containing 23 specific items of information about the franchise offering, its officers, and other franchisees [www.ftc.gov].

Required franchise disclosure topics under the Franchise Rule include, among others, the franchise's litigation (lawsuit) history, past and present franchisees and their current contact information, any exclusive territory that comes with the franchise, the assistance the franchisor provides franchisees, the cost of purchasing and starting up a franchise and, if a franchisor makes representations

139

about the financial performance of the franchise, this topic also must be covered in the disclosure document. Further, the material basis for a franchisor's representations must be revealed to the potential franchisee. Typically, these franchise disclosure topics are referred to collectively as the **Uniform Franchise Offering Circular ("UFOC"),** and they are followed in most states with their own state franchise disclosure laws.

Prior to the enactment of the Federal Trade Commission's (FTC's) Franchise Rule of 1978, the state of California began its movement to regulate franchise offerings during the decade of the 1960s. Before these franchise rule disclosures went into effect, the franchise industry had a terrible reputation and an image of tremendous hype, little to no substance, and a complete absence of management talent. The one consistent common denominator that these early franchisors had was tremendous talent in their salespeople.

"Scamming" has a long and rich history in the franchise industry.

For example, some of the franchise offerings of the 1950s, 1960s and 1970s were for companies that had never even opened a single store or unit prior to selling franchises to the public. Many had so-called "management" that has little to no experience in the business being offered by the franchisors, but had too much experience in bankruptcies of their previous businesses, lawsuits, and problems with regulators. Quite frankly, they were bandits.

Many of these early franchises were so financially feeble that they needed the proceeds from the franchise sales in order to meet current payroll, to pay for the advertising the prospects had responded to, and to pay other past due and currently due bills. Even with more government regulation today, however, there are still numerous franchise offerings that are such pitiful opportunities that they remind us of the old days of no regulation [www.ftc.gov; money.howstuffworks.com; online.wsj.com].

A. 30 Secrets or Tips for Avoiding Franchise Scams

1. Get your copy of the Franchise Disclosure documents, as required by the FTC's Franchise Rule, immediately. Do not spend your money on a franchise that the franchisor cannot, or will not, provide you a complete disclosure document for. No exceptions.

2. Study the disclosure document carefully, and ask questions of the franchisor.

3. Go online, on the Internet, and research the franchisor. Look for postings, news stores about the franchisor, filings for and against the franchisor, etc. Study the franchisor company's website.

4. Likewise with 3, above, research carefully the industry that the franchisor is allegedly a part of. Decide what the franchisor's standing, if any, is in the industry. Compare it to its competition in the industry (franchised or non-franchised).

5. If the franchisor company is "public" (sells stock to the public), research the information available about it from the company's Securities and Exchange Commission filings, and from state filings.

6. Learn as much as you can about the franchisor's management. Thoroughly research the backgrounds of management.

7. Locate and visit some of the franchisor's stores or units . . . some of its franchisees. Talk to the franchisees. Ask questions.

8. Ask the franchisor about the process it (or they) use in selecting franchisees. If you get the sense that the franchisor does <u>not select</u> franchisees, but instead is in the business of <u>selling</u> franchises, be cautious. This indicates substantial risk to the franchisee.

9. Remember: Any franchisor who is willing to <u>sell</u> its franchises without other due diligence requirements of (i) insisting that the potential franchise visit its headquarters and (ii) some of its other franchisee locations, (iii) as well

as engage in a mutual interview process, is probably a very risky franchise.

10. If the franchise salesperson you are dealing with or talking to is <u>not</u> a franchise employee but instead an outside salesperson, this is another sign of a risky franchise. An outside salesperson (broker) doesn't get paid unless he or she makes the sale; and, since he or she has no long-term stake in the franchise, they essentially are without interest as to whether the new franchisee fails. In sum, outside salespersons (franchise brokers) typically move on to the next franchisor looking to sell franchises to anyone with the money.

11. When you visit the franchisor's headquarters (which is a <u>must</u>), meet and speak with as many of the franchise support people as you can. Ask questions.

12. Assess and evaluate each and every employee (management and support staff), and gain a measure of their experience to do their jobs. Make as many contacts as you can.

13. Evaluate headquarters, and every office you enter. Does headquarters look and feel successful? Or, do you get a sense of gloom and doom? Is the company's money at headquarters being used for "lights and brights" (expensive items such as marble, brass, furniture, and luxuries), or does it appear that the company is investing its resources in useful items such as competent personnel, training programs, computers, and other useful support components.

14. Make sure you are very confident that the franchisor has the necessary experience in the business or field being offered in the franchise.

15. As part of your evaluation of management and support staff, be sure they have a history of success in the particular business, first; and, if not, how about their track of success in a related business? Evaluate carefully. Call or check on their past track record with other businesses.

16. What is the real financial condition of the company? Speak with the chief financial officer, personally. Does the franchise have a history of profitability?

17. Make the tough decision, after careful and thorough consideration, whether you are getting the proper and/or expected value for your monetary investment. If capable, also try to make a judgment as to whether your emotional and physical input will pass the cost-benefit analysis for the franchise.

18. Check on the franchisor's litigation and/or regulatory history. Franchisors are required to disclose their relevant litigation history. Litigation is not necessarily bad. In fact, sometimes it is good. Any franchisor of any size that enforces system standards will occasionally need to sue some franchisees. The key is whether they (the franchisors) are able to still maintain good relationships with their other franchisees while engaging in litigation against offenders. If so, the franchisor may be able to maintain an aura of strong and responsible leadership. As always, however, litigation should be the last resort for the franchisor as well as the franchisee.

    However, to be clear, several pages of lawsuits from franchisees against the franchisor are <u>not</u> a good sign. The potential franchisee should make every effort to understand the basis for these franchisee (as well as franchisor) lawsuits, and make a decision based upon the facts. Hire a knowledgeable attorney to help with this process; preferably an attorney very familiar with franchising and with the particular industry.

19. Determine whether the franchise offering is made <u>only</u> in the "non-registration" states. This is important because, if a franchisor is offering franchises all over the United States, with the exception of the twelve (12) "required registration" states, this may be an indication that the franchise does not meet the more stringent requirements of the twelve (12) required-registration states. Be very careful of this situation [Actually, franchisors are required to register in 15 states; but in Florida, Nebraska and Texas, franchisors may file for exemptions].

Either you or your attorney should be able to acquire a list of the twelve (12) franchise registration states from, for instance, the International Franchise Association (IFA) in Washington, D.C., at (202) 628-8000; or the Bureau of Consumer Protection, Federal Trade Commission (FTC), in Washington, D.C.

20. Determine which professional organizations the franchisor belongs to, such as the Better Business Bureau, the International Franchise Association (IFA), etc.

21. Hire competent professional help in the form of lawyers, accountants, and franchise experts knowledgeable in the industry you are seeking to join, and so forth.

22. **Beware of the "Rented Rolls-Royce Syndrome."** Avoid franchisors whose representatives are overdressed, super-flashy, and work overtime to impress you with an appearance of super-success. Stick with and study the franchisor's Uniform Franchise Offering Circular. Make sure you have a copy of the franchisor's updated audit report to read [Caffey, Andrew A., "How To Spot A Scam," www. enterpreneur.com/franchises].

23. **Do not be "hustled."** Avoid franchisors whose sales representatives use the following types of sales pitches to get you to buy: "Time to buy is fast running out!," "Our franchise territories are selling out quickly!," "It's now or never!," "Make a decision now or it will be too late!." These franchisors are trying to hustle you.

24. **Avoid "Cash Only" Transactions when purchasing a franchise**. If you make a payment of any type, make it out in a check to a company, not to an individual. This way you can stop payment, etc.

25. **Avoid the "Greed Appeal."** If it sounds too good to be true, it usually is too good to be true. Avoid the boasting franchisor and its sales representatives. Be prepared to write your own business plan, or hire someone you trust to competently do so for you.

26. **Location, Location, Location.** The right location is "everything" in franchising. Make sure you have nailed down the right location for your franchise before you join or buy.

27. **Avoid the "Lazy Theme" Franchisor.** Any successful franchise takes time, work, and effort. I have never seen a franchise of which the consumer just paid the money and then sat o his or her hands and watched the money come in. This is a pipe dream.

28. **Avoid the "financially anemic" franchisor.** Study the UFOC carefully, and, in consultation with your accountant and your attorney, make sure the franchisor is adequately capitalized to fulfill its contractual obligations to you.

29. **Royalty fees over franchise sales.** In consultation with your accountant, check to make sure you are comfortable with the amount of money the franchisor is making from royalty fees (the franchisor's allotted percentage of its franchisee sales) over and above its franchise sales [www.franchiseprospector.com].

30. **In consultation with a competent franchise expert, evaluate to make sure the franchisor is offering you a business model that really works.** Make sure the franchisor's business model has been successfully time tested before you join the system.

B. **12 Signs of a Good Franchise Opportunity**

1. The professionals you have hired to assist and advise you regarding the franchise opportunity—that is, your attorney, accountant, and franchise expert—all agree that the opportunity is good!

2. All legal and regulatory filings and registrations are complete and in order for the franchisor, including the franchise disclosure documents.

3. At least three (3) years of the franchisor's (i) financial statements and (ii) legal history indicate sound financial and legal management.

4. Industry growth and market research on the franchisor's industry is positive, according to your own research as well as that of the franchisor. Check particularly on these indicators in your specific geographic market of interest. For example, an ice cream franchise may not have a good market in northern Alaska; but, if not saturated too much, may find a good market in southern Florida.

5. The ongoing unit or franchise growth is good. The franchisor's name and brand recognition is growing positively.

6. The franchisor provides strong support to its franchisees in terms of training, franchising (perhaps), and other assistance.

7. The franchisor has good management and support staff; with good training and experience in franchising and in the product or service industry.

8. The franchisor provides good advertising and marketing support to its franchisees. One of the bigger complaints of many franchisees is the perception of inadequate advertising and marketing support (which the franchisees pay for) from the franchisor.

9. The franchisor's franchisees are satisfied, or preferably even happy, with their system. There are few, if any, lawsuits between the franchisor and its franchisees.

10. The franchisees are able to make an adequate, and preferably good, living from the franchise. Many franchisors provide potential franchisees with "average earnings" information in their Franchise Disclosure Documents (FDD).

11. The franchisor responds promptly, straight-forwardly, and honesty to the franchisees' questions and concerns.

12. And finally, the franchise and the franchisor are good fits for the franchisee. The franchise and the franchise culture are

a good fit with the franchisee's personality, skills, interests, and even passion.

[www.franchising.com; www.franchise.org; www.ftc.gov]

If interested, here's hoping that you find a good franchise opportunity for you.

<u>Summary</u>: Chapter Fourteen—Franchising-Opportunities and Scams

1. The Federal Trade Commission's (FTC's) "Franchise Rule," originally enacted in 1978, is the primary Federal law which governs franchising in the United States. The Rule requires franchisors (sellers of franchises) to provide potential franchisees (purchasers of franchises) with an extensive Franchise Disclosure Document (FDD) containing 23 specific items of information about the franchise offering, its officers and management, and other franchisees [www.ftc.gov]. Study this document carefully before joining or purchasing a franchise.
2. Since the 1950s, "scamming" has had a long and rich history in the franchise industry.
3. Do not join or purchase a franchise that does not require a due diligence investigation of the franchisor (seller of the franchise) by the potential franchisees (purchaser of the franchise).
4. When considering the purchase of any franchise, make sure you have secured the services of a qualified attorney, competent accountant, and franchise expert to assist you.

Chapter Fifteen

Contract Law for the Consumer

*If the consumer remembers nothing else about contract law,
he or she should remember this: When it comes to written or
printed contracts, generally the BOLD (large) print giveth
and the FINE (small) print taketh away.*

If you are a consumer who is about to make a major purchase,
or pay for services, this chapter should be helpful to you.

In law, a contract is a binding legal agreement that is enforceable
in a court of law or by binding arbitration. A contract, in other
words, is a lawful exchange of promises with a specific legal remedy
for breach (or violation).

Contracts can be oral (verbal) or written; however, some contracts
are required by their nature to be written **[Ware, Charles Jerome,
Understanding The Law: A Primer, p. 57 ("Four Basic Guides
to Contracts"), 2008].** Generally, in most states, the contracts that
are required to be in writing are called "Statute of Frauds" contracts.
Read them very carefully.

"Statute of Frauds" Laws

Typically, both written and oral contracts are enforceable by
law. Generally, however, most states have laws which mandate
certain types of contracts to be in writing. These state laws are called
"Statute of Frauds" laws since their primary purpose is to prevent
fraudulent claims.

The phrase or term "statute of frauds" goes way back several centuries to an English Act of Parliament (29 Chas. 2 c. 3) passed in 1677. The Act was authored by Sir Leoline Jenkins and passed into law by the Cavalier Parliament. It was officially called "An Act for Prevention of Frauds and Perjuries." From this old English act, the Statute of Frauds emerged with the requirement that certain kinds of contracts are memorialized in a signed writing.

Historically, in common law tradition, the Statute of Frauds could be remembered by the mnemonic **"MY LEGS,"** meaning:

— Marriage,
— One Year,
— Land,
— Executor,
— Goods, and
— Surety.

In other words, historically the Statute of Frauds required a writing signed by the parties (or, at least the defendant) in the following circumstances:

M = Contracts in consideration of marriage;
Y = Contracts which cannot be performed within one year;
L = Contracts for the transfer of an interest in land;
E = Contracts by the executor of a will to pay a debt of the estate with his own money;
G = Contracts for the sale of goods above a certain value (today, this value is usually $500); and
S = Contracts in which one party becomes a surety (i.e., acts as guarantor) for another party's debt or other obligation.

Typically, although the laws vary from state to state, a Statute of Frauds contract should:

— Identify the parties entering the contract;

149

— Make the contract identifiable by spelling out the subject matter; and
— Give the fundamental terms and conditions of the parties' agreement.

It should be noted that even when a <u>written</u> contract is not required, it is a good idea to have one anyway; since it may be difficult to prove that an oral agreement existed, and there may remain questions regarding the terms of the agreement.

Consumer Contract Laws

Consumer contract laws provide consumers protection in the general marketplace by making sure consumers have the fundamental information they need about a product or service. This allows consumers better opportunities to make informed decisions before purchasing products and services.

Federal and state laws require that all information and facts concerning a consumer contract transaction be fully disclosed to the consumer. The primary intent and goal behind these Federal and state laws is to promote balance between consumers and sellers of products and services in the marketplace. This proposed balance is accomplished primarily by mandating the seller to reveal any terms or conditions that apply to the sale of the goods or services [ehow.com/consumercontractlaws].

Consumer Cancellation Rights

Depending upon the state you are in, a number of laws give consumers a legal right to cancel contracts in certain specific transactions within a relatively short time period after the consumer signs the contract. And, this cancellation can occur without the consumer giving the seller or other party a reason for the cancellation or even having to show "legal cause."

It is important to note that many "cancellation periods" are measured in "business days" (interpreted usually as Monday through Friday). There are usually no penalties for cancelling by the consumer under these cancellation laws. However, the consumer's cancellation typically must be in writing and delivered to the seller within the time period permitted by the cancellation law. Frequently, though, the consumer's notice of cancellation is effective when it is deposited in the U.S. mail with proper address and postage. It is recommended that the consumer have proof of the mailing to the seller.

Depending upon your state law, consumer cancellation rights may apply, for example, for the following goods and services:

— Time Share purchases (frequently 3 business days)
— Dance Studio classes and services;
— Automobile sales;
— Dating Services;
— Discount Buying Services
— Credit Repair Services
— Door-to-Door Sales
— Home Improvement Contracts;
— Mail or Telephone Sales;
— Mortgage Foreclosure Consultant Services;
— Weight-Loss Services; and so forth.

Federal Trade Commission (FTC)

The Federal Trade Commission is considered the primary agency for protecting U.S. consumers from unfair and deceptive business practices. As part of this mission, the FTC provides no-cost information to consumers to educate the public on how to avoid becoming victims of contract inadequacies, fraud, deception, misleading advertising and pricing tactics.

Just about every state has consumer contract laws and regulations that are designed to enhance consumer confidence in the marketplace. Many states based their consumer contract laws on the Federal Trade Commission's regulations and enforcement.

The Attorney General for each state is usually the primary official enforcing that state's consumer protection regulations.

Even though the language of the consumer contract protection statutes vary from state to state, all have the generally expressed goal and purpose of protecting consumers from unfair and deceptive business practices related to the sale or lease of merchandise, services or property. Most state statutes often provide conventional breach of warranty cases and usually cover a wide variety of industries; from automobile and airlines to time shares, utilities and sweepstakes. [www.ftc.gov/bcp]

FOUR (4) CONTRACT CLAUSES TO BEWARE OF

There are four (4) particular contract clauses that I strongly recommend the consumer be aware of:

1. The Confessed Judgment Clause. A confession of judgment clause is usually contained in a note signed by the borrower and is included to authorize the creditor to obtain a judgment against the borrower without providing advance notice to the debtor. The confessed judgment clause is usually "slipped into" the note or agreement by the creditor. If the unfortunate debtor "defaults," the creditor simply files, generally, a complaint in confession of judgment in court and issues an execution against the debtor's assets. This action could effectively change an unsecured interest of the creditor into a second interest [resource.slawinfo.com].

    I do not like confessed judgment clauses, and I strongly recommend that the consumer or borrower be very cautious about signing agreements that include them [And see, "definitions.uslegal.com/c/confession-of-judgment"].

2. The Arbitration Clause. Arbitration, in a nutshell, is the process in which the opposing sides to a legal dispute agree to hire another person (a substitute for a judge) to listen to their arguments in a less formal setting and render a decision on the

matter (like a judge) for them [see, **Charles Jerome Ware, Understanding the Law: A Primer, p. 16 (2008)**].

It is my observation that arbitration tends to favor the more well-heeled party to the dispute. Therefore, I am not very optimistic about its use for disputes involving the average consumer. Arbitration can also be expensive for the parties.

An "arbitration clause" is commonly used in a number of consumer contracts such as credit cards, stock brokerages, and so forth. The clause may or may not specify the jurisdiction or venue for the arbitration, but it always binds the parties to a type of resolution outside of the court system.

With respect to resolving disputes between the average consumer and companies (merchants), I typically do not recommend arbitration. In fact, I generally feel that the average consumer is disadvantaged by the process.

3. The Hold Harmless Clause. This provision in a contract relieves a party or parties to the contract from liability, either as a matter of negotiated agreement, or in the event that circumstances beyond his or her control prevent them from fulfilling the terms of the contract. [www.teachmefinance.com/financial].

As an example, in a home construction loan, the lender may agree by contract to hold the borrower harmless in the event that the home construction was not completed on time due to a worker strike or other catastrophe, thus preventing the lender's foreclosure on the loan.

In sum, the hold harmless clause indemnifies the parties to a contract on a unilateral or reciprocal basis, as the case may be [www.businessdictionary.com/definition/hold-harmless-clause].

This clause can be bad or good for the consumer, depending upon the factual circumstances. In any event, though, it should be thoughtfully considered by the consumer prior to agreeing to it. Consulting with an attorney and other relevant professional is highly recommended as part of the consideration process.

4. The Liquidated Damages Clause. This clause in a contract allows for payment of a specific amount (damages) agreed upon

by the contracting parties in case of breach (violation) of the contract. These damages go to the injured party to collect as compensation upon the specific breach of the contract [West Encyclopedia of American Law, www.answers.com/topic/liquidateddamages].

Liquidated damages clauses are commonly used in real estate contracts. For real estate buyers, liquidated damages clauses can limit their losses if they default (violate the contract). For sellers, liquidated damages clauses provide a preset amount of money, usually the buyer's deposit funds, in a timely manner to the seller if the buyer defaults. Liquidated damages clauses have the advantages to parties in a contract of (i) mutual agreement on damages upon default and (ii) predictability of damages involving costs, among others. Consulting with an attorney and other relevant professional is highly recommended in considering liquidated damages.

Summary: Chapter Fifteen—Contract Law for the Consumer

1. If you remember nothing else about contract law, remember this: When it comes to written or printed contracts, generally the BOLD (large) print giveth and the FINE (small) print taketh away.
2. Even when a contract is not required to be written (pursuant to the Statute of Frauds or otherwise), it is a good idea for the parties or participants to have a written contract anyway; since it may be difficult to prove that an oral agreement existed, and there may remain questions regarding the terms of the agreement.
3. In deciding whether a contract must be in writing, remember the Statute of Frauds mnemonic: "MY LEGS." (Marriage; one Year; Land; Executor; Goods; and Surety).

4. Federal and state laws require that all information and facts concerning a consumer contract transaction be fully disclosed to the consumer.

5. A number of state laws give consumers a legal right to cancel contracts in certain specific transactions within a relatively short time period after the consumer signs the contract. And, this cancellation can occur without the consumer giving the seller or other party a reason for the cancellation or even having to show "legal cause" [check with an attorney for legal advice on this issue and other topics related to this].

6. Four (4) particular contract clauses that the consumer should be aware of and review carefully are:

    (a) The Confessed Judgment Clause

    (b) The Arbitration Clause:

    (c) The Hold Harmless Clause; and

    (d) The Liquidated Damages Clause.

Chapter Sixteen

Secrets and Tips for Avoiding Debt Collection Harassment

For many years now, the dreaded debt collectors have been the most complained-about industry on the Federal Trade Commission's (FTC's) consumer website. What's worse is the fact that serious abuses by out-of-control debt collectors are getting worse everyday.

Particularly for vulnerable older consumers, debt collection abuse and harassment can take a terrible toll [www.consumerlaw.org/issues/seniors].

The bad news is that this industry is getting worse. The good news is that there are Federal and state laws that are specifically designed and intended to protect consumers from debt collection abuse and harassment.

These Federal and state laws apply and are enforceable regardless of whether or not the consumer actually owes money on the alleged debt being collected. The problem is that too many of these vulture-like debt collectors do not comply with these laws unless the consumers file complaints against them.

The purpose and goal of this chapter is to empower the consumer with secrets and tips to avoid debt collector abuse and harassment. The information provided will not only help the consumer directly, it will also assist consumer advocates in counseling clients about what a debt collector can and cannot do in pursuing consumer debt.

A. What is the worst a creditor can really do to a consumer?

The National Consumer Law Center (NCLC), a non-profit organization dedicated to "protecting vulnerable consumers and promoting marketplace justice," maintains very helpful information on its website for consumers who may be victims of debt collection abuse and harassment; particularly for seniors in our society [http://www.consumerlaw.org/issues/seniors]. NCLC addresses this issue adeptly and helpfully.

In reality, a debt collector for a creditor has no more authority than to demand payment from the consumer for the creditor. The steps a debt collector takes to demand payment from the consumer can become problematic, and will be addressed further in this chapter. Meanwhile, if the creditor has not repossessed or otherwise taken the consumer's house, or car, or boat, or other property as collateral for the debt, then the creditor can legally do only about three (3) things:

1. Stop doing business with the consumer;
2. Report the alleged default to a credit bureau (who, by the way, frequently get the information wrong; <u>see</u>, Chapter Three, <u>supra</u>);
3. File for arbitration resolution, or file a lawsuit in court. Frequently this arbitration/litigation threat may not be as serious as many consumers believe. For various reasons, many creditors do not follow through on their threats. Further, even if they do arbitrate or sue, consumers can raise defenses to paying the debt.

Arbitrating or suing, and the collecting on a judgment, are separate steps. A judgment does not necessarily force the consumer to pay the debt. The judgment only gives the creditor the legal right to attempt to collect on the debt from the consumer; usually by attempted garnishment on the consumer's wages or attachment (lien) on the consumer's other property.

157

B. The Federal Trade Commission (FTC) and the Fair Debt Collection Practices Act (FDCPA).

Remember: If a debt (bill) collector oversteps the bounds of Federal and state law, the consumer does have recourse against him or her.

The Fair Debt Collection Practices Act (FDCPA), 15 U.S.C. § 1692, prohibits certain debt (bill) collectors from engaging in abusive, unfair, or deceptive behavior to collect from the consumer. The Act covers debt (bill) collectors who regularly collect debts owed to others. These collectors include collection agencies, lawyers who collect debts on a regular basis, as well as companies that purchase delinquent debts and then attempt to collect them [www.ftc.gov/bcp/edu/pubs/consumer/credit]. The Act does not cover debt collectors that are employed by the original creditor (the business or person who first extended the loan or credit). However, if a debt collector that works for a collection agency breaks the law, the consumer <u>can</u> take steps to make sure it does not happen again.

The Federal Trade Commission (FTC) enforces the Fair Debt Collection Practices Act (FDCPA). The Act covers personal, family, and household debts including money the consumer owes on a personal credit card account, an auto loan, a money bill, and mortgage. The FDCPA does not cover debts the consumer has incurred to run a business.

C. What Debt (Bill) Collectors Cannot Do.

Debt (Bill) Collectors from collection agencies <u>cannot</u> do any of the following:

<u>Harassment</u>. Debt collectors may not harass, oppress, or abuse you or any third parties they contact. For example, they may not:

— use violence against the consumer;
— use threats of violence or harm;

— publish a list of names of people who refuse to pay their debts (but they can give this information to the credit reporting companies);_
— use obscene or profane language; or_
— repeatedly use the phone to annoy someone;
— call you repeatedly or contact you at an unreasonable time (the law presumes that before 8 a.m. or after 9 p.m. is unreasonable).
— place telephone calls to you without identifying themselves as bill collectors; or
— contact you at work if your employer prohibits it (and most employers do prohibit it).

<u>False Statements</u>. Debt collectors may not lie when they are trying to collect a debt. For example, they may not:

— falsely claim that they are attorneys or government representatives;
— falsely claim that you have committed a crime;
— falsely represent that they operate or work for a credit reporting company
— misrepresent the amount you owe (claim the consumer owes more than they do);
— indicate that papers they send you are legal forms if they aren't; or
— indicate that papers they send to you aren't legal forms if they are.

Debt collectors also are prohibited from saying that:

— you will be arrested if you don't pay your debt;
— they'll seize, garnish, attach, or sell your property or wages unless they are permitted by law to take the action and tend to do so; or
— legal action will be taken against you, if they do so would be illegal or if they don't intend to take the action.

Debt collectors may not:

— give false credit information about your to anyone, including a credit reporting company;
— send you anything that looks like an official document from a court or government agency if it isn't; or
— use a false company name.
— send you a paper that resembles a legal document.
— Add unauthorized interest, fees, or charges.
— Contact third parties, other than your attorney, a credit reporting bureau, or the original creditor, except for the limited purpose of finding information about your whereabouts.

Unfair Practices. Debt collectors may not engage in unfair practices when they try to collect a debt. For example, they may not:

— try to collect any interest, fee, or other charge on top of the amount you owe unless the contract that created your debt or your state law allows the charge;
— deposit a post-dated check early;
— take or threaten to take your property unless it can be done legally; or
— contact you by postcard.

D. The Eight (8)-Step Process: Consumer Practices to Avoid Abuse and Harassment.

Remember: Even though Federal law applies only to third-party debt (bill) collectors, some states also have laws which cover creditors that collect their own debts. Check with your state's Attorney General's Office or other Consumer Protection Agency. In the meantime, consumers should consider the following eight (8)-step process in avoiding debt (bill) collector abuse and harassment.

1. <u>Negotiation and Discussion</u>. Try to negotiate and discuss the debt problem with the creditor <u>before</u> the creditor refers the debt out to a collection agency. The consumer should consider calling up the creditor to explain their difficult financial situation.

    Do not "over-promise" to the creditor during these negotiations.

    Think carefully before promising anything to the creditor, what your defenses are to the debt, or to part of the debt.

2. <u>The "Cease and Desist" Letter</u>. Write the debt (bill) collector a "cease and desist" letter requesting that the bill collector stop their collection abuse and harassment.

The FDCPA generally mandates that collection agencies stop their collection efforts (frequently called "dunning" efforts) upon receipt of the consumer's "cease and desist" letter. Although self-collecting creditors (those creditors collecting their own debts) are not covered by the FDCPA, these creditors often will still honor the consumer's letter.

The consumer should remember to keep a copy of the written "cease and desist" request letter, and to send the original to the agency or creditor by self-proving methods (certified mail-return receipt; priority mail-confirmation; courier, etc.) to have proof of delivery.

A SAMPLE "Cease and Desist" LETTER follows:

Charlie Bee Consumer
8 Debtor Lane
Drowning, MD 21040

February 1, 2010
Dread Collection Agency
91 Insane Avenue
Drowning, MD 21039

Dear Sir or Madam:

I am writing to request that you stop contacting me about an account number _____ with [name of creditor] as required by the Fair Debt Collection Practices Act 15 U.S.C. section 1692c(c). (Note: Delete reference to the Act where the letter is to a creditor instead of to a collection agency. Some, but not all, state laws prohibit further contact by creditors).

[Describe any harassing contact by the collection agency. If appropriate, provide information about why you cannot pay the bill or do not owe the money].

This letter is not meant in any way to be an acknowledgement that I owe this money. I will take care of this matter when I can. Your cooperation will be appreciated.

Very truly yours,
Charlie Bee Consumer

Consumers should keep careful records and copies of all correspondence to and from creditors and collection agencies.

3. The Legal Letter (aka, "The Lawyer's Letter").
   Should the consumer's "cease and desist" letter fail to stop the debt (bill) collection calls, a well-crafted letter from an attorney frequently will suffice. In his or her letter, the attorney often may be able to raise legal claims and defenses on the consumer's behalf and highlight violations of Federal law (usually the FDCPA) that prohibits the debt collector's activities.

   Federal law (the FDCPA) requires collection agencies to stop contacting or communicating with a consumer known to be represented by an attorney, as long as the attorney responds to the collection agency's inquiries. Though not mandated by the FDCPA, even creditors collecting their own debts will usually abide by requests to "cease and desist" from a consumer's lawyer. And certainly, pursuant to legal ethics, an attorney representing a creditor or collection agency should not contact the consumer-debtor directly who is known to be represented by an attorney.

4. Negotiate, Negotiate, Negotiate. Most collection agencies usually have some leeway to negotiate with the consumer. As always, I caution the consumer to studiously avoid "over-promising" to the collection agency during these negotiations.

5. Billing Errors and Other Defenses Should be Raised by the Consumer as promptly as detected. The consumer-debtor always has the right (and, indeed, responsibility) to request corrections in their bill when the consumer believes mistakes have occurred. Further, pursuant to the FDPCA and many state laws, collection agencies must inform consumers of their right to dispute the alleged debt; usually during the first contact or communication with the consumer or within five (5) days after the first contact or communication. Generally, by law, the consumer has thirty (30) days after this initial contact from the collection agency to dispute the debt in writing. The collection agency then must stop collection efforts while it investigates

the dispute debt. Disputes by the consumer involving a line of credit, a credit card, or an electronic transfer of money are required as well to be investigated by the creditor.

6. File Complaints with the Appropriate Federal and State Government Agencies. Consumers may file complaints for debt collection abuse and harassment with the Consumer Protection Bureau of the Federal Trade Commission (FTC), the appropriate State's Attorney General's Office, or other appropriate Consumer Protection agency.

   Letters of complaint should be sent to the Consumer Response Center at Federal Trade Commission, CRC-240, Washington, D.C. 20580. Consumers can also call the Commission toll-free at 1-877-FTC-HELP (382-4357) or file a complaint on-line at www.ftc.gov. Copies of the letter should also be sent to the consumer protection division within the state Attorney General's office, usually in the state capitol, and also to any local office of consumer protection listed in the local telephone book or on the Internet. Addresses can be obtained from a local Better Business Bureau or Office of Consumer Affairs.

7. Bankruptcy. Not the best option or strategy where the consumer's only concern is debt collection abuse and harassment. But, effective.

   Bankruptcy is an effective and powerful tool because it stops immediately all collection efforts and activity by debt collectors, creditors, and frequently even government agencies. This extraordinary remedy of bankruptcy should be reserved for situations when consumers have very serious financial problems. Do not pull the trigger too quickly on this option, and, by all means, consult with a bankruptcy attorney before choosing to file bankruptcy.

8. Lastly, File a Lawsuit against the Offending Debt (Bill) Collector for Unlawful Conduct. Generally, the consumer has the right to file a lawsuit in a Federal or state court within one year after the date the law (FDPCA, etc.) was violated.

Should the consumer prevail in the lawsuit, the judge can require the debt collector to pay the consumer for any damages he or she can prove they suffered because of the illegal collection practices. Damages, among other things, can include medical bills and lost wages. Further, the judge can require the debt collector to pay the consumer up to $1,000.00, even if the consumer cannot prove that he or she suffered actual damages.

The consumer can be reimbursed for his or her attorney's fees and court costs. A class action lawsuit including a group of similarly-situated consumer-victims may also be brought to recover money for damages up to $500,000.00, or one (1) percent of the debt collector's net worth, whichever amount is lower.

Debt collection abuse and harassment does not, however, void a legitimate debt owed.

E. Consumer Income Exempt from Garnishment.

Ultimately, if the debt is proven to be legitimate and the consumer does not pay it, the creditor or debt collector can sue the consumer, get a judgment, and attempt to collect on the judgment.

Attempts by creditors to collect on judgments against debtors usually involve two (2) mechanisms: (i) attachment (lien) against personal and real property, and (ii) garnishment of the consumer-debtor's wages and/or other income.

Not all of a consumer-debtor's wages and/or other income can be garnished, however. Many Federal benefits, for examples, are exempt from garnishment, including:

(1) Social Security Benefits
(2) Supplemental Security Income (SSI) Benefits
(3) Veterans' Benefits
(4) Civil Service and Federal Retirement and Disability Benefits
(5) Service Members' Pay
(6) Military Annuities and Survivors' Benefits
(7) Student Assistance

(8) Railroad Retirement Benefits

(9) Merchant Seamen Wages

(10) Longshoremen's and Harbor Workers' Death and Disability Benefits

(11) Foreign Service Retirement and Disability Benefits

(12) Compensation for Injury, Death, or Detention of Employees of U.S. Contractors Outside the U.S.

(13) Federal Emergency Management Agency Federal Disaster Assistance

But Federal benefits may be garnished under certain circumstances, including: to pay delinquent taxes, alimony, child support, or student loans.

<u>Summary</u>: Chapter Sixteen—Secrets and Tips for Avoiding Debt Collection Harassment

1. Keep your debt problems in perspective. The worst a creditor generally can do to a consumer, other than repossession and foreclosure on property, is to (a) stop doing business with the consumer, (b)) file a legal action (lawsuit or arbitration) against the consumer, or (c) report the consumer's default to a credit bureau.

2. The consumer does have recourse against abusive and harassing debt collectors by way of Federal and state laws, and private legal action.

3. The definition for debt collector "abuse or harassment" is relatively and appropriately broad, and generally provides the consumer with several options ("The Eight (8)-Step Process") for relief.

4. Do not "over-promise" to the creditor or debt collector when discussing or negotiating payment or settlement of your debt.

5. Document everything when dealing with harassing and abusive creditors and debt collectors.

6. Four (4) names to remember and invoke when dealing with abusive and harassing creditors and debt (bill) collectors are:

    (a) The Federal Trade Commission;
    (b) The Attorney General's Office;
    (c) The Fair Debt Collection Practices Act (15 U.S.C. Section 1692); and
    (d) My Attorney.

7. There are at least thirteen (13) Federal benefits (sources of income) that are exempt from garnishment; with the exception that Federal benefits may be subject to garnishment under the following four (4) circumstances: (i) to pay delinquent taxes, (ii) alimony; (iii) child support, and (iv) student loans.

Chapter Seventeen

Recognizing and Avoiding Tax Debt Settlement Scams

If the promise or pitch sounds too good to be true, it probably is too good to be true.

If the promise or pitch of settling a consumer's tax debt for literally pennies on the dollar sounds too good to be true, it probably is too good to be true.

Although there are thousands of legal and accounting professionals who regularly advocate for their clients for lower tax bills, there are many so-called "tax debt settlement firms" coming on-stream everyday with advertisements and promises of aggressive tax representations and outrageous results. Many of these firms are unscrupulous scammers.

The promise of these firms include client access to veteran tax professionals (such as "former IRS officials") capable of solving the taxpayer's IRS problems with enormous talent and experience, and a vast array of legal, accounting and financial tools [www.bankrate.com/finance/taxes/tax-scam]. In truth, for the most part, these so-called "tax settlement specialist" or "veteran tax professionals" are actually selling the tax client the effort of one tax strategy: the **Offer in Compromise (OIC) process**.

The IRS's "Offer in Compromise (OIC)" process is legitimate, but the average tax payer's chances of getting the relief expected or even promised by these firms are minimal or even remote.

What is an 'Offer in Compromise?"

An "offer in compromise" (OIC) is an agreement between the taxpayer and the Internal Revenue Service (IRS) that settles the taxpayer's liabilities for less than the full amount allegedly owed [IRS.gov; www.irs.gov].

Like most creditors, the IRS knows that not all taxes owed will be paid. Therefore, rather than allowing a legitimate tax debt to become uncollectible, the IRS will negotiate and accept less tax money than is owed in certain circumstances [www.bankrate.com/finance/taxes]. However, absent these certain or special circumstances, an office in compromise will not be accepted or negotiated if the IRS believes or concludes that the tax liability can be paid in full by the taxpayer either as a lump sum or through a payment agreement.

The fact is that the IRS will not accept an offer in compromise (OIC) unless the amount offered by the taxpayer is either equal to or greater than the "reasonable collection potential" (RCP) for the tax debt and the taxpayer. This is true regardless of which so-called "tax debt settlement" company the taxpayer hires.

The "reasonable collection potential" (RCP) is the procedure or process the IRS uses to measure the taxpayer's ability to pay the tax debt, and includes the value that can be realized from the taxpayer's assets, such as real estate (realty), automobiles, bank accounts, and other personal property (personalty). The RCP also includes anticipated future income minus certain accepted amounts allowed for basic living expenses. Promises by so-called "tax debt settlement" firms of settling IRS claims for "pennies on the dollar" are simply unrealistic under most circumstances.

The IRS may negotiate and accept an offer in compromise (OIC) based on three (3) grounds:

(i) <u>Doubt as to Collectability</u>. Sufficient doubt exists that the taxpayer could ever pay the full amount of the tax liability owed within the remainder of the statutory period of limitations for collection.

(ii) <u>Doubt as to Liability</u>. A sufficient doubt exists that the assessed tax liability is accurate; and

(iii) <u>Effective Tax Administration</u>. There is no doubt that the tax liability is correct or valid and there is potential to collect the full amount of the tax owed, but at least one exceptional circumstance exists that allows IRS to consider an OIC.

Fifteen (15) Secrets and Tips for Recognizing and Avoiding Tax Debt Settlement Scams

1. Ask knowledgeable professionals about the reputation and track record of the so-called tax debt settlement firm you are considering.
2. Be wary of firms (providers) that claim (or appear) to only or mostly do offer in compromise (OIC) work.
3. Research the prospective firm on the Internet; and add the word "scam" to your search to learn more of the complaints and experiences of other consumers.
4. If you believe you qualify for an OIC, and believe you are capable (to request it), try to do it yourself first.
5. Be reasonable and realistic. If the price of hiring a so-called "specialist" is expensive (several thousand dollars, for instance), question yourself as to whether pleading hardship to IRS will work for you. In other words, do your own cost-benefit analysis.
6. Be cautious if during your initial interview or meeting with the tax debt specialist he or she does not ask you the fundamental question of whether you feel you owe the tax debt. The issue of whether you truly owe the tax debt should be important to a true professional, and to you as taxpayer.
7. If the company's promises, or its pitch to you, sounds too good to be true, it probably is too good to be true. Be wary of the company that "over promises" great results for you. This should be a red flag. Even the most skilled tax professionals cannot make the IRS accept many offers of settlement from some taxpayers.

8. Be wary of the companies that advertise so much you instantly know their name.

9. Likewise, be cautious about any firm that promises your tax problem will be resolved quickly. The OIC process is slow. Period.

10. It is not a good sign that your contact person in the company changes regularly. You should be able to get to know this person fairly well, and vice versa.

11. Be careful if your first required deposit of many to engage the company's services oddly reflects how much cash you have available (or tell them you have available).

12. Steer clear of tax debt settlement firms that use "phantom" offices. Google, Bing, or otherwise locate the company's offices on the Internet. Look for drop box situations, mailing addresses without real offices, etc.

13. Be very suspicious if you have difficulty reaching or contacting your representative or "specialist" after you have paid money to the firm to represent you. Bad sign.

14. Find out who you know, or who they know, who has used the company before; or, is presently using the company's services; in other words, engage in due diligence.

15. Trust your own instincts about the firms. Go with your gut reaction . . . your instincts. If the situation does not feel right to you, there is a good chance it is not right for you.

Summary: Chapter Seventeen.
Recognizing and Avoiding Tax Debt Settlement Scams

1. In truth, what most so-called "tax debt settlement specialists" or companies are selling the tax client is just one (1) tax reduction strategy or process: the Offer in Compromise (OIC).

2. The average taxpayer's chances of getting the tax relief they want or expect from these alleged tax debt settlement "experts" is minimal or remote.

3. Beware of "over-promising" by the alleged tax debt settlement company. If the company's promises or marketing pitch to you sounds too good to be true, they probably are too good to be true. Some examples of "over-promising" by these firms include: "We can probably settle your tax debt for pennies on the dollar;" and "We should be able to get this process resolved for you immediately."

4. When judging or trying to decide the state or condition of the economy, I recommend the consumer look more at "Main Street" (his or her local economy) than "Wall Street", which is certainly important but sometimes more remotely connected to the consumer's personal economic or financial condition.

Chapter Eighteen

Dealing with Government Agencies

Government agencies can be difficult at times to deal with:

"God's Original Claim"

A New Orleans lawyer sought a Federal Housing Administration (FHA) loan for a client. He was told the loan would be granted if he could prove satisfactory title to a parcel of property being offered as collateral. The title to the property dated back to 1803, which took the lawyer three months to track down. After sending the information to the FHA, he received the following reply.

(Actual reply from FHA):
"Upon review of your letter adjoining your client's loan application, we note that the request is supported by an Abstract of Title. While we compliment the able manner in which you have prepared and presented the application, we must point out that you have only cleared title to the proposed collateral property back to 1803. Before final approval can be accorded, it will be necessary to clear the title back to its origin."

Annoyed, the lawyer responded as follows:
(Actual response):

"Your letter regarding title in Case No. 189156 has been received. I note that you wish to have title extended further than the 206 years covered by the present application. I was unaware that any educated person in this country, particularly those working in the property area, would not know that Louisiana was purchased by the United States from France in 1803, the year of origin identified in our application. For the edification of uninformed FHA bureaucrats, the title to the land prior to U.S. ownership was obtained from France, which had acquired it by Right of Conquest from Spain. The land came into the possession of Spain by Right of Discovery made in the year 1492 by a sea captain named Christopher Columbus, who had been granted the privilege of seeking a new route to India by the Spanish monarch, Queen Isabella. The good Queen Isabella, being a pious woman and almost as careful about titles as the FHA, took the precaution of securing the blessing of the Pope before she sold her jewels to finance Columbus's expedition. Now the Pope, as I'm sure you may know, is the emissary of Jesus Christ, the Son of God, and God, it is commonly accepted, created this world. Therefore, I believe it is safe to presume that God also made that part of the world called Louisiana. God, therefore, would be the owner of origin and His origins date back to before the beginning of time, the world as we know it, and the FHA. I hope you find God's original claim to be satisfactory. Now, may we have our damn loan?"

[SOURCE: bounce-9003652-93975@lists.trialsmith.com (Jack Condliffe)]

The Federal Housing Administration, generally known as "FHA", is one of many government agencies at the Federal, state and local levels. This particular federal government agency provides mortgage insurance on loans made by FHA-approved lenders throughout the United States and its territories.

Government Agencies

By definition, purpose and even their history—government agencies can be difficult at times to deal with. They do operate differently, on the hold, than most people realize or think. Government agencies are permanent or semi-permanent organizations within the bureaucracy or machinery of government that are responsible for the oversight and administration of very specific functions.

Recommendations for the Consumer when contacting a government agency:

1. Go online, read an appropriate brochure or encyclopedia, or ask a knowledgeable person—but learn at least a little about the government agency before contacting it. In sum, do a little research on the agency before contacting it. <u>Why?</u> (See <u>2</u>, next).
2. Why? Because it is very important that you contact the <u>correct</u> or <u>proper</u> agency for your specific issue<u>.</u> <u>Remember!</u> (See <u>3</u>, next).
3. No government agency has all of the answers for you; and each government agency has very limited answers in very specific areas of inquiry.
4. There are no "one-stop, one-shop" government agencies for all answers in any area of expertise.
5. Be patient and courteous with the government employee you are seeking assistance from, for the following reasons:

    (i)   "Honey gets more attention and relief than vinegar". Be nice in seeking assistance. Do not intentionally alienate or aggravate the government employee.
    (ii) In many cases, the consumer has contacted the wrong agency for relief anyway, and the employee is simply trying to be helpful without the proper knowledge;
    (iii) Usually the offended government agency employee will have the "last laugh" on a rude, impatient or discourteous consumer;
    (iv) Sometimes, the government agency employee does not have the proper answer or response for the consumer. Impatience and discourtesy probably will not make the employee more knowledgeable or helpful.
    (v)   Always try to elicit the identification of the government agency employees you are speaking with. Try honey instead of vinegar to get the identifications.

(vi) <u>REMEMBER:</u> The structure, design and organization of government agencies are not based upon "commonsense", <u>per se</u>. They are based upon "purpose" and "goal". Understand the purpose and goal of the agency . . . and you will be more effective in dealing with it.

<u>Summary:</u> Chapter Eighteen—Dealing with Government Agencies

1. Generally government agencies, like most large bureaucracies, operate a lot differently from you and I as individuals. Therefore, their actions can frequently not make a lot of sense to us as constituents and consumers. Be methodical, purposeful, and patient with them.

Chapter Nineteen

Avoiding Debtors' Prison
In The United States

Debtors Prison

"The confinement . . . of any man in the sloth and darkness of a prison, is a loss to the nation, and no gain to the creditor. For, of the multitudes who are pining in those cells of misery, a very small part is suspected of any fraudulent act by which they retain what belongs to others. The rest are imprisoned by the wantonness of pride, the malignity of revenge, or the acrimony of disappointed expectation." [www.samueljohnson.com/debtrsp./idler#22 (September 16 1758)]

Scenario: You, the consumer, have not committed a crime, but a law enforcement officer is looking for you with an arrest warrant. The problem: You owe a debt.

Brief History of Debtors' Prisons

Historically, a "debtors' prison" is a jail for those people who are unable for some reason to pay a debt. Before the mid-19th century or so debtors' prisons were a common method or instrument for dealing with unpaid debts [see, Lucinda Cory, "A Historical Perspective on bankruptcy", On the Docket, Volume 2, Issue 2, U.S. Bankruptcy Court, District of Rhode Island, April/May/June 2000; http://en.wikipedia.org/wiki/Debtors'Prison; "Timeline: A Brief History of Bankruptcy", The New Times, 11-16-2005].

In the early Roman Republic, a person could pledge himself or herself as collateral for a loan. This loan agreement was called a "nexum". If the debtor failed to pay the debt, he or she was liable to become the creditor's slave. This "nexum" contract arrangement was voided in or about 326 BC by Roman leader Lex Poetelia Papiria. Later, during Europe's Middle Ages, both men and women debtors were jailed together in a single large jail cell until their families or friends could pay their debt [Ibid].

Debtors' Prisons in the United Kingdom (Great Britain, et al.) were popularized for a long while by the Fleet and King's Bench Prisons, and written about by the great English writer, Charles Dickens, in his novels. The Debtors Act of 1869 abolished imprisonment in England for debtors who could not pay; however, debtors who clearly had the means to pay their debt, but simply did not do so, could still be incarcerated for up to six weeks [http:// www.charles-dickens.com/CharlesDickensBibliography; "In Prison For Debt", Manchester Times, Manchester, England, October 22nd, 1862].

In Greece, a debtor can still be imprisoned for not paying his or her debt to a private bank. Germany still maintains comparable concepts to debtors' prisons. Debtors in the United Arab Emirates (including Dubai) can be imprisoned for failing to pay their debts. China, including Hong Kong, has debtors' prisons, inter alia [Wayne Arnold, "How The World Is Dealing With The Issue of Debtors", The National (December 24, 2008), www.thenational.ae/apps/ pbcs.dll/article; "Debtors' Prison Awaits Deadbeats In hong Kong", February 5th, 1984, http://news.google.com/newspapers; "In Hong Kong, Some Debtors Still Go To jail", May 8th, 1983, www.nytimes. com (New York Times); "Debtors Could Face Jail Time", December 16, 2009, China Economic Review, www.chinaeconomicreview. com/today-in-china/2009; Robert F. Worth, "Laid-Off Foreigners Flee As Dubai Spirals Down", The New York Times, December 12, 2009, www.nytimes.com; www.berlinonline.de/Berliner-zeitung/ archive/.bin/dump.fcgi; www.reporto.gr/news.asp].

In 1976, Article 11 of the International Covenant on Civil and Political Rights (ICCPR) was enacted, stating: "No one shall be imprisoned merely on the ground of inability to fulfill a contractual obligation".

And finally . . . the **United States:**

For a longtime in the early history of the United States, the use of debtors' prisons in this country was a widespread practice. Even two prominent signatories to the Declaration of Independence, Robert Morris and James Wilson, were later sent to debtors' prison in the United States. It is reported that by 1816, more than two thousand New Yorkers annually were incarcerated in debtors' prisons in that state alone. In Virginia, Henry Lee III, also known more popularly as "Light Horse Harry Lee"—a top Revolutionary War general, former prominent Governor of the Commonwealth of Virginia, and beloved father of the great Confederate general Robert E. Lee—was imprisoned as a debtor for one year in Montross, Virginia when his son, Robert, was two years old [Wendy McElroy, "The Return of Debtors' Prison?", www.independent.org/newsroom/article, April 1st, 2008; Jill Lepore, "I.O.U.", New Yorker, April 13, 2009, www.newyorker.com/reporting; http://leeboyhoodhome.com].

Sometimes, in the earlier days of the United States, people were incarcerated in debtors' prison for less than sixty cents ($0.60) worth of debt! [John B. McMaster, The Acquisition of Political, Social and Industrial Rights of Man in America, Cleveland, Ohio: Imperial Press, page 63 (1903, ISBN 978-1409771876)].

In 1833, the United States finally abolished Federal imprisonment of debtors for unpaid debts ["Timeline: A Brief History of Bankruptcy, The New York Times, November 16th, 2005].

Imprisonment for debt was abolished in New York in 1831. Most other states in America followed and abolished the practice in or around the same period of 1831 to 1834 [see, supra, Wendy McElroy and Jill Lepore].

Debtors' Prison in the United States

Pay up . . . or be locked up. Debtors' prison in the United States has resurfaced.

Most unfortunately, in the United States today, in the year 2011, the use of incarceration to collect debts is becoming increasingly popular. So much so that many lawmakers, lawyers, judges and regulators are attempting to restrict or curb the United States debt collection industry's unfortunate use of arrest warrants to collect debt owed by consumer borrowers who are delinquent on credit card payments, automobile and boat loans, and other bills [see, "Welcome to Debtors' Prison, 2011 Edition", The Wall Street Journal, WSJ.com, March 17, 2011].

Over 33% of all American states allow sanctions of incarceration against consumer borrowers who either cannot or will not pay their debts. This action is usually called civil contempt.

For instance, the following nine (9) states permit debt collectors to seek arrest warrants for consumer debtors who are in default, if the debt collector can show that all other lawful collection methods have failed:

— Arkansas
— Arizona
— Illinois
— Indiana
— California
— Michigan
— Alabama
— Minnesota, and
— Washington State.

Generally, the consumer debtor is arrested, taken into custody, and ordered to submit financial documentation to the courts to make it easier for the creditor to seize the consumer's assets or garnish the consumer's wages. However, in some cases the debtor may even be held indefinitely until a payment plan or agreement is reached. Or, particularly if the debtor is insolvent, until the debt is paid in full [see, www.startribune.com/local; "Welcome to Debtors' Prison, 2011 Edition", WSJ.COM, March 17, 2011].

Other states, including Tennessee and Oklahoma, have held this practice of debt collection by incarceration to be illegal (and, indeed, unconstitutional) [see, Oklahoma State Constitution 2, §13].

Almost universally within the United States, however, child support obligations and delinquencies are an exception to the "no debt collection by incarceration" practice. In fact, courts and law enforcement agencies in several states frequently arrest so-called "dead-beat" parents for failing to pay their child support ["Jail for child support", www.ajc.com, December 15th, 2010]. Many elected law enforcement officials frequently make a "show" of it.

The Wall Street Journal reports that judges in nine different counties in New York state have ordered more than five thousand arrest warrants at the behest of the debt collection industry since the beginning of 2010 and until march of 2011, covering a total population of about 13.6 million New York state-area residents. Further, interviews of about twenty judges nationwide reveal the number of consumer debtors threatened with arrest in their courtrooms has grown substantially since the financial crisis began in or about 2008 ["Welcome to Debtors' Prison, 2011 Edition", WSJ.COM, March 17th, 2011].

In contradiction to the thousands of arrests which occur in the United States each year of consumer debtors on behalf of creditors, the fundamental premise still remains in theory:

In the United States, it is still supposed to be unconstitutional to incarcerate a person solely for failing to pay a debt.

[see, "Debtors' Prison—Again", St. Petersburg (Florida) Times, www.tampabay.com/opinion/editorial/article, April 14, 2009; "Timeline: A Brief History of Bankruptcy", The New York Times, November 16th, 2005; "Is Jailing Debtors The Same As Debtors Jail?", startribune.com, June 9th, 2010; "The New Debtors' Prisons", The New York Times, www.nytimes.com, April 6th, 2009.

The devil, then, is in the details.

Debtor arrests are usually couched or hidden in the format of creative nuances or instruments such as *(i) violations of court orders, (ii) violations of probation or parole, (iii) etc.*

"BAD CHECK" Criminal Prosecutions

The increasing use of "bad check" state criminal prosecutions to collect civil obligations in many jurisdictions has become a topic of controversy among legal scholars. Generally, in these types of criminal prosecutions to collect debts the bad check defendant (the accused debtor) is provided the choice of making restitution (paying the debt) to the creditor, or going to criminal trial and facing possible jail time for having written and tendered the bad check (insufficient funds) to pay a debt [Kratsch & Young, Criminal Prosecution and Manipulative Restitution: The Use of State Criminal Courts and Contravention of Debtor Relief, Ann. Surv. Bank L. (1984); quoting "imprisonment for debt has once again become a reality"].

As far back as 1986, the United States Supreme Court decided that a restitution order in a criminal prosecution for welfare fraud was <u>not</u> discharged in subsequent bankruptcy by the debtor even though there was a failure of the restitution obligor (creditor) to act to exempt the debt from bankruptcy discharge [Kelly v. Robinson, _U.S._, 107 S. Ct. 353 (1986).]

As expected, people who go to jail for not paying their debts end up owing even more money when they are released from jail. The reason is obvious: they have not earned any money during their incarceration.

Some Techniques for Avoiding Debtors' Prison in the United States

1. Document EVERYTHING when dealing with your creditors. "Document" means in writing. Remember: Documentation . . . Documentation . . . Documentation. Telephone calls are insufficient for documentation concerning debt collection.

2. Keep a FILE on your debts. File everything. Good record-keeping and filing is a major PLUS.

3. If you are behind in your payments to your creditor/lender, periodically write (document) notes and letters to your creditor outlining in summary fashion your legitimate and earnest reasons for your delinquency. Keep and file your copies of all correspondence.

4. If your financial circumstances are unfortunate and honest, make them known to your lender.

5. Always COMPLY with court orders.

6. If you cannot comply, for good reason, with court-ordered payments, be sure to inform the court in writing—preferably before a petition or notice or complaint of non-compliance is filed against you.

7. Always COMPLY with parole and/or probation orders.

8. If you cannot comply with parole and/or probation orders, be sure to inform your parole and/or probation office (and/or the court) immediately. This technique applies to payments as well as other requirements of your parole and/or probation.

9. Immediately REPORT any debt collection agency or company that threatens to have you arrested for a debt (non-payment of a debt) to these agencies:

    — The Consumer Protection Bureau (Bureau of Consumer Protection, or BCP) of the U.S. Federal Trade Commission (FTC);
    — The Better Business Bureau (BBB);
    — The Attorney General's Office for your State (State AG); probably the AG's consumer protection division; and
    — Any other consumer agency or appropriate law enforcement agency.

10. If you legitimately cannot afford to pay your child support, file with the court to modify, amend, or reduce it immediately.

11. Certainly when you are threatened with arrest for a debt, contact a lawyer immediately.

12. Do not write bad checks.
13. Always acquire a state-registered or state-certified license to do work such as home improvement projects for money. Frequently, you can be pursued in a criminal prosecution to seek restitution for the customer if you are an <u>unlicensed</u> vendor [<u>see</u>, Chapter 12, <u>supra</u>, "Home Improvement Consumer Secrets and Tips"].

<u>Summary</u>: Chapter Nineteen—Avoiding Debtors' Prison In The United States

1. The United States abolished Federal imprisonment of debtors for unpaid debts in 1833.
2. Over 33 percent of all American states allow sanctions of incarceration against consumer borrowers who either cannot or will not pay their debts.
3. Almost universally within the United States, child support obligations and delinquencies are an exception to the "no debt collection by incarceration" practice.
4. Debtor arrests are usually couched or hidden in the format of creative nuances or instruments such as (i) violations of court orders, (ii) violations of probation or paroles; (iii) etc.
5. For instance, the following nine (9) states permit debt collectors to seek arrest warrants for consumer debtors who are in default, if the debt collector can show that all other lawful collection methods have failed:

— Arkansas
— Arizona
— Illinois
— Indiana
— California
— Michigan
— Alabama
— Minnesota, and
— Washington State.

Generally, the consumer debtor is arrested, taken into custody, and ordered to submit financial documentation to the courts to make it easier for the creditor to seize the consumer's assets or garnish the consumer's wages. However, in some cases the debtor may even be held indefinitely until a payment plan or agreement is reached. Or, particularly if the debtor is insolvent, until the debt is paid in full.

6. Always acquire a state-registered or state-certified license to perform for pay work such as home improvement projects for others. Frequently, you can be pursued in a criminal prosecution to seek restitution or damages for the customer if you are unlicensed [see, Chapter 12, supra, "Home Improvement Consumer Secrets and Tips"].

Chapter Twenty

Concluding Thoughts

"Life in America is exclusively economic [and financial] in structure and lacks depth" [By German Historian Oswald Spengler; Peter Stearns, Consumerism in World History: The Global Transformation of Desire (Themes in World History), 2nd Edition, Routledge, Taylor and Francis Group; 2001, 2006].

"American materialism [is] a beacon of mediocrity that [threatens] to eclipse [the mediocrity of] French civilization" [By French Writer Georges Duhamel; Ibid].

"Our enormously productive economy demands that we make consumption our way of life, that we convert the buying and use of goods into rituals, that we seek our spiritual satisfaction and our ego satisfaction in consumption. We need things consumer, burned up, worn out, replaced and discarded at an ever-increasing rate" (1955) [By Economist Victor Lebow; http://hundredgoals.files. wordpress.com/2009/05/journal-of-retailing].

The United States is a nation of consumer, built upon the social and economic order of consumerism, which places an emphasis on consumption in ever greater amounts [Thorstein Veblen (1899); The Theory of the Leisure Class: An Economic Study of

<u>Institutions</u>, Dover Publications, Mineola, New York, 1994, ISBN 0486-28062-4; consumerism,answers.com].

There are some who consider "consumerism" to be the "biggest religion" in America; surpassing Evangelical Christianity, mainstream Protestantism, and even Catholicism [see, "Rev. Billy: High Priest of Frugality", article on Rev. Bill Talen, http://money.msn.com/how-to-budget/reverendbilly]. Consumerism, according to popular evangelist Rev. Bill Talen, is the deeply held American belief that "buying stuff makes us better and happier . . . that purchases can fill the voids in our hearts and souls" [Ibid]. Therefore, opines "Rev. Billy", consumerism makes Americans stand in line, sit in traffic, and causes us to buy several unnecessary products just to take each other on a date [Ibid].

Consequently, the United States also is a nation of debtors . . . consumer debtors. Within recent years in this country, consumer debt issues have consistently been near or at the top of the consumer complaints nationwide. Because Americans buy and spend so much, we acquire heavy debt. This year, 2011, in most states throughout this country, the top three (3) consumer complaints include:

(1) Mortgage Foreclosures
(2) Debt Collection Agencies, and
(3) Credit Card Companies.

[see, www.walletpop.com/2011/03/03/debt-issues-top-list-of-consumer-complaints; www.thedigteratilife.com].

In an effort to avoid economic and financial problems, consumers must be more knowledgeable. Absolutely, the best consumer is the informed consumer [see, www.agingcarefl.org/aging/consumerproblems]. From personal injury and medical malpractice to mortgage loans and credit cards, the wisdom remains the same: **consumer knowledge is consumer power.**

You have been exposed to a wealth of consumer legal information, tips, and secrets in this book. The average consumer would probably, at this time, need suggestions to get started on the road to consumer empowerment. Therefore, let me make the following cursory suggestions in closing:

1. Unwanted or unsolicited faxes. Remove yourself from unsolicited or unwanted advertising fax lists. Many of these solicitations can be tempting or intriguing, but very few are worthwhile offers. The Federal law which specifically covers the consumer's rights in these circumstances is the Telephone Consumer Protection Act [47 U.S.C.S. §227 (2001)]. This Act includes "telephone communications", "telephone facsimiles", and "unsolicited advertisements" among its offenders. The Act, as well as many states' laws, allow lawsuits to be pursued under this statute in state courts, including small claims court, to stop (enjoin) such actions.

   The Telephone Consumer Protection Act (the "Act") provides for compensatory damages of up to $1500 for each unsolicited fax if it is proven that the fax advertiser acted knowingly and willingly; and it permits punitive damages of $500 for each unsolicited fax. To set up his or her case, the consumer should inform the fax advertiser offender (I strongly recommend this be done in writing) of the Act and of the Consumer's rights, and warn the offender that if the offender continues to send the unsolicited faxes the consumer intends to pursue his or her rights under the Act [www.identitytheftsecrets.com].

2. Do not accept or participate in unsolicited or unwanted commercial telephone calls. Hang up. You do not have to be nice when hanging up on these people.

3. Add yourself to the National "Do Not Call" Registry [https://www.donotcall.gov/default.aspx]. You can accomplish this by either going online (see, previous internet site) or calling (888-382-1222). Telemarketers rarely have anything worthwhile to offer the consumer.

4. Routinely Check Your Social Security Statement.

   Your personal Social Security Statement provides a record of past earnings and estimated future benefits based on things such as retirement or disability. The Social Security Administration recommends checking your statement at least once every three years. I strongly recommend you check your Statement <u>every year</u>. When you don't check your Statement for several years, it becomes problematic in disputing any errors on it, particularly errors in earnings [Call 800-772-1213, or go to www.ssa.gov/mystatement; or go to https://secure.ssa.gov/acu/IPS].

5. <u>Destroy</u> (if by Mail) or <u>erase</u> (if by Internet) all unrequested or unsolicited offers of credit or loans. You know why, having read this book. Most of these so-called "offers" are bogus.
6. <u>Reject all requests</u> for your personal information from solicitors. By now, having read this book, you know why. It is extremely dangerous to give your personal information to solicitors.
7. <u>Remove your name from marketing lists</u>. These lists can be very harmful to you and your finances.

These lists are "traps" for your valuable personal information. Resist this temptation. To start, call the credit bureaus "opt out" telephone number at 888-5optout (888-567-8688).

You also can write the "Big 3" credit agencies and instruct them <u>not</u> to share your personal information for any type of marketing purposes. Current addresses for the three major credit card companies to send your "opt out" letter to are:

(i)   Equifax, P.O. Box 105, Atlanta, GA 30348-0241; Phone: 800.685.1111.
(ii) Experian, P.O. Box 2104, Allen, TX 75013-2104; Phone: 888.397.3742.
(iii) Trans Union, P.O. Box 390, Springfield, PA 19064-0390; Phone: (800)916-8800.

Hold the "Big 3" accountable by way of the FTC credit complaint process.

Make sure you keep a copy of your letter for your own files. The following is a sample letter to use as a guide for your own "opt out" letter:

To Whom It May Concern:

RE: Opt Out of Disclosure of My Personal Information

I hereby opt out of the sale, rental, distribution, exchange or other disclosure of any and all personal information you have about me. This includes but is not limited to my name, home address and phone, work address and phone, work address and phone, email addresses, social security number, driver's license number, financial account and access numbers and my transaction history with you. Please promptly confirm in writing that you will not disclose my personal information without my expressed consent.

Full Name: _____

Signature: _____

Address:_____Date: _____

8. File Complaints. Get in the habit of filing complaints against offending companies for unlawful business practices, identity theft, or other commercial improprieties. This includes filing complaints against the "Big 3". The United Nations is a nation of consumers, built upon receiver and investigator of consumer complaints [https://www.ftccomplaintassistant.gov; http://www.ftc.gov/pphonefraud; and see, Federal Communications Commission, http://www.fce.gov/cgb/policy/TCPA]. Other agencies for the consumer to file complaints with include states' attorney general offices, the Better Business Bureau, and many state, local, and Federal consumer protection offices [see, previous chapters in this book].

The fact that you are reading this book indicates that you are a consumer who wants to be better informed. That is a good thing. Our desire and wish is that this book has been, and will be, of help to you and other consumers in becoming more informed. You can do it.

Thank you for this opportunity to serve you.

Summary: Chapter Twenty—Concluding Thoughts

1. You do not have to be nice when hanging up on unsolicited callers, especially commercial solicitors.
2. Most unsolicited offers are bogus or not worthy.
3. Hold the "Big 3" credit bureaus accountable by way of the FTC credit complaint process.
4. Add yourself to the National "Do Not Call" Registry (1-888-382-1222).
5. Reject all requests for your personal information from solicitors who call, fax, or confront you in person.

PART III

SUMMARY: LEGAL CONSUMER TIPS AND SECRETS

SUMMARY

Legal Consumer Tips and Secrets

—Avoiding Debtors' Prison in the United States—

<u>Chapter One: Personal Injury 101</u>

1. Be aware and be patient. Too many consumers who are victims of personal injury settle their cases too soon; without full and proper medical treatment and physical rehabilitation.
2. Every personal injury claim or lawsuit has to be filed within a certain time period or time limit, called a "statute of limitations" period. Each and every state has a "statute of limitations" period for various offenses.

<u>Chapter Two: Medical Malpractice 101</u>

3. No matter how egregious or awful the facts may seem in a potential medical malpractice case, credible expert medical testimony is necessary to make the case.
4. In general, there are no guarantees of medical results.

<u>Chapter Three: Credit Bureaus, Credit Scores and the Credit Business</u>

5. Credit collection is a multi-billion dollar business annually; very big business.
6. Credit collection is legalized invasion of privacy. Credit agencies are always digging up personal information on consumers.

7. Currently, the "Big 3" major credit bureaus are Equifax, Experian, and TransUnion. They are private companies, <u>not</u> government agencies. They make lots of money.

8. Lawsuits the consumer is involved in may be on his or her credit report even if the consumer did not lose the case.

9. Credit reports are frequently wrong . . . to the consumer's detriment. The major interest of credit bureaus is to make money, not report your credit properly.

10. Credit reports, generally, are biased against the consumer. An affinity or propensity by the credit reporting agencies is to seek, find, and report what negative data they can get on the consumer. They are <u>not</u> particularly concerned with the consumer's positive credit information.

11. The alleged one "credit score" for each consumer or person is a myth. Among the major credit reporting agencies there can be several different "credit scores" for each individual.

12. The predominant so-called "credit score" software algorithm (complex mathematical formula) used by the "Big 3" major credit reporting agencies in the United States—Equifax, Experian, and TransUnion—is called FICO, named after the company that developed it: Fair Isaac Corporation.

13. FICO was developed by a company headquartered in Minneapolis, Minnesota by the name of Fair Isaac Corporation (or FICO). It is a multi-billion dollar financial services company company with over 2,000 employees.

14. Your FICO score is inherently unfair since, among other reasons, it is proprietary (money-making) and thus is treated as a secret. Therefore, no consumer or individual has the capacity to compute his or her own FICO score.

15. Generally, your FICO credit score cannot be lower than 300 nor higher than 850.

16. Oddly, FICO history and track records show that, ideally, a credit score in the 800s is probably not any better for the consumer's credit position than a credit score in the 700s. In other words, a credit score higher than the 700s will probably

not increase significantly the average consumer's credit attractiveness to lenders.

17. Your credit score does not reflect your overall financial picture. Though important in our society, your credit score does not reflect your income, employment history or your assets. It certainly reveals little about your character.

18. Even if you pay off your credit card every month it does not necessarily increase your credit score or make you a lower credit risk. Hmmm . . . Go figure.

19. Since a crucial point in credit worthiness and credit reporting is how much available credit the consumer has used on his or her card, it is important to remember that it looks better for the consumer when computing their FICO credit score if the consumer uses less than half of their credit limit.

20. Since it is believed that about 30% of the consumer's FICO credit score is based upon so-called "credit utilization," taking advantage of popular "reward cards" or "reward programs" can and does affect the consumer's creditworthiness . . . and can be hurtful credit-wise for the "rewards" enthusiast.

21. It is recommended that the consumer keep his or her balances lower by cutting back on his or her credit use for about two months or so before applying for major purchase loans such as a new mortgage or car loan. This step should help improve your credit score.

22. Late payments are believed to account for about 35% of your total FICO credit score, even though you may have since paid the debt in full.

23. It is true that negative information will frequently stay on your FICO credit report for up to 7 years.

24. Positive credit information can remain on your FICO credit report for longer than seven years.

25. Generally, if you have positive credit information on your credit report, it is recommended that you leave it there. Presumably, the good credit history adds to your creditworthiness long-term.

26. Generally, free credit reports are worth about what you pay for them: nothing. These free reports rarely, if ever, reflect or show the so-called "real" scores that lenders request and see. Free credit reports tend to be more frightening than helpful.

27. "Soft" credit score inquiries should not affect you FICO credit score. These inquiries are the ones in which (i) you check on your score, (ii) your current lender checks your credit, (iii) some potential lender allegedly "pre-approves" you for credit, among others. By the way, there is no such thing as "pre-approval" for credit.

28. "Hard" credit score inquiries can, and frequently do, negatively affect your FICO credit score. These inquiries occur when (i) you apply for a loan or credit, (ii) you open a bank account, (iii) you make a major purchase such as a home or car, among others. Everytime you request or ask for credit, you are punished by a "hard" credit score inquiry.

29. It is recommended that the consumer ask straight forwardly at the beginning if a bank, insurance company, or automobile dealer, etc., intends to check his or her credit record. Multiple "hard" credit inquiries over a period of several weeks could hamper the consumer's credit score for a year or more.

30. In general, credit cards should be treated as your enemy; not your friend. They can be convenient in our lives, but they are not truly necessary for most consumers.

31. The United States Federal Trade Commission (or FTC) considers itself to be the premier protector of the American consumer; and, in particular, American consumer credit reporting rights. It is the FTC that administers the federal Fair Credit Report Act (FCRA), to promote accuracy, fairness, and privacy of consumer credit information.

32. Among other requirements, the Fair Credit Reporting Act (FCRA) mandates each of the nationwide consumer reporting companies—currently Equifax, Experian and TransUnion—to provide the consumer with a free copy of his or her credit report, at the consumer's request, once every (12) months.

33. For more information on consumer credit report rights, visit the following website: www.ftc.gov/credit; or write:

> Consumer Response Center
> Federal Trade Commission
> Room 130-A
> 600 Pennsylvania Avenue, N.W.
> Washington, D.C. 20580

34. The law requires that the consumer must be informed if information in the credit file has been used against them.
35. The law gives the consumer the right to know what is in his or her credit file.
36. The law gives the consumer the right to request and receive his or her "credit score" from each credit reporting agency.
37. The law gives the consumer the right to dispute any and all incomplete and inaccurate information in their credit file or report.
38. The law requires that consumer reporting agencies correct or delete inaccurate, incomplete, or unverifiable information found in the consumers' credit file, usually within 30 days of notice of this information.
39. The law requires that consumer reporting agencies not report "outdated" or "outmoded" negative information.
40. By law, access to the consumer's credit file is limited. In other words, not everyone is allowed access to your personal credit information.
41. By law, consumer credit reports cannot be given to the consumer's employers or potential employers without the consumer's prior written consent.
42. The law permits consumers to sue for damages against violators if harmed by violations of his or her credit rights.
43. If you are active duty military or a consumer identity theft victim, the law grants you additional rights under the Fair Credit Reporting Act (FCRA). See, www.ftc.gov/credit.

Chapter Four: Fifteen (15) Tips for Avoiding Foreclosure

44. Remember the phrase "Produce the note" when facing foreclosure. The lender must produce it in order to complete the foreclosure. Consult a qualified attorney or other professional about this issue.

45. Some experts have predicted or assessed that upwards of forty percent (40%) of mortgage notes cannot be produced by the mortgagor or lender upon demand. Production of the mortgage note is generally required by law.

46. Nationwide, courts generally have responded favorably to the "produce the note" strategy.

47. Beware of tax consequences with the "short sale" as well as the "deed in lieu of foreclosure".

48. With effort from the consumer, in most instances foreclosure can be avoided.

49. The law requires that the lender send the consumer a formal "Notice of Default" prior to taking any further foreclosure action against the consumer.

50. After receiving a "Notice of Default," if the consumer pays the full amount owed on the mortgage within the specified time limit, and then continues timely payments, the lender is prohibited by law from taking further action against the consumer.

51. Many states allow a "period of redemption after foreclosure and sale" in which the consumer has the opportunity to redeem their home and buy it back.

52. Believe it or not, legitimate lenders do not want your house. Too much trouble; not their line of business. Many lenders, therefore, have options for consumers to help them through difficult financial times. Foreclosing on your house can be quite problematic for the lender.

53. Foreclosure scams and schemes are numerous in our society. Avoid them. Contact a lawyer or other qualified housing professional for advice prior to getting involved with so-called

foreclosure prevention companies or foreclosure recovery scams and schemes.

Chapter Five: Avoiding Identity Theft and Identity Fraud

54. Adopt a "need to know" approach to revealing your personal information. Be stingy about giving out your personal information to others in any form, manner, or fashion.
55. Check on all of your personal financial information on a regular basis, including credit reports, bank statements, credit card statements, and so forth. Do not just "glance" at these documents or this information; review it carefully.
56. For identity theft purposes, I recommend the consumer collect and retain his or her monthly or period financial statements and checks for at least 3 years.

Chapter Six: Work-At-Home Scams and Schemes

57. A general rule to remember is that real or legitimate employers pay the employee, not the other way around. If the consumer is asked to pay for work of any type, and particularly, work-at-home jobs, just say "no."
58. If the work-at-home opportunity sounds too good to be true, it usually is too good to be true.
59. Always investigate or research the potential work-at-home employers thoroughly.

Chapter Seven: From Charles Ponzi to Bernard Madoff: The "Ponzi" and other Investment Schemes

60. The "Ponzi" scheme relies upon greed. It is a fraudulent investment operation that pays irrationally high returns to early investors from their own money and/or from money paid by later investors; rather than from any actual profit earned from products or services.

61. Ponzi schemes can be very enticing to the investor—particularly the early investor, but they are doomed to fail. The Ponzi system is destined to collapse because the alleged earnings, if any, are always less than the payments to investors.

Chapter Eight: The Affinity Scam

62. The Bernard Madoff Ponzi case is the classic example of "Affinity fraud." Affinity fraud refers to scams that prey upon <u>fellow</u> members of identifiable groups, such as racial or ethnic groups, the elderly or professional groups, fraternal or sororital groups, and so forth. In other words, the Ponzi is identified as a member of the victim group.

63. Regardless of <u>how</u> the investment scheme comes to your attention (whether by family member or other relatives, friends, colleagues, religious group members, or anyone else who inspires a bond of trust or confidence), if the scheme looks or sounds too good to be true, it probably <u>is</u> too good to be true.

Chapter Nine: Four (4) Things Not To Do When You Are In Debt

64. Do not rely solely on "minimum" or "minimal" payments or small monthly payments on your cards to improve or even maintain your credit rating.

65. Be cautious about rolling your debt balance or credit card balance over to an introductory rate credit card.

66. Never assume your interest rates are constant or the same.

67. Be wary of debt settlement scams and schemes.

Chapter Ten: Avoiding Debt Settlement Scams

68. "Debt Settlement" is <u>not</u> the same as "Debt Consolidation."

69. More so than debt consolidation, debt settlement usually involves (i) unsecured debt, (ii) that generally will, to some degree, be "charged off" (R-9 on your credit report), and (iii)

that most likely will require that the consumer be issued a 1099 from the creditor on the debt that is settled.

70. Be very cautious about debt settlement companies that require money upfront from the consumer without providing a precise, personalized plan of action that is specifically tailored to the individual consumer's financial situation.

71. Sometimes, even frequently, debt settlement may not be the best choice for the consumer. If that's the case, the debt settlement company should be capable, willing, and honest enough to advise the consumer accordingly and offer alternatives or options to the consumer.

72. Look for the legitimate and reputable debt settlement companies that offer a written guarantee (or "money-back guarantee") to the consumer. These companies do exist in this industry.

73. If what the debt settlement firm says sounds too good to be true, then it probably is too good to be true (see 76, below).

74. Generally, a good debt settlement company can be expected to save the consumer, on average, from 40% to 60% on his or her debts.

75. Before signing-up with the selected debt settlement company (or, for that matter, before any agreement in writing) read the contract carefully. (See, 78, below).

76. Remember: The Bold (large) print in a contract giveth, and the Fine (small) print taketh away!

Chapter Eleven: The "Nigerian," The "Singapore," The "Irish Lottery," and Other Internet Scams

77. Scams pop-up on the Internet from all nations and nationalities on a daily basis. They rely on consumer greed for their success.

78. These types of Internet offerings usually promise an exorbitant amount of money, amounting to unrealistic expectations on the part of the consumer victims.

79. Remember: If the Internet offering looks or sounds too good to be true, it usually is too good to be true. Avoid greed.

Chapter Twelve: Home Improvement Consumer Secrets and Tips

80. The average consumer should be very cautious about doing business with any company that pursues him or her "too aggressively." Home improvement schemers are known for their aggressiveness; including door-to-door fliers, street corner signs, "cold" calling, etc.
81. Be sure to hire a <u>licensed</u> home improvement contractor.
82. Many states have a Guaranty Fund (the Fund) for consumer victims that is established by assessments to licensed contractors. The Fund compensates homeowners for actual monetary losses due to poor workmanship or failure to perform a home improvement contract by a <u>licensed</u> home improvement contractor.
83. Always make sure changes to your home improvement contract are in writing.

Chapter Thirteen: Dark Secrets of Credit Cards and Debit Cards

84. Debit cards and credit cards can be dangerous to the consumer's financial health; particularly since they are types of "electronic money" with high fees and risks associated with their use. "Electronic money" is dangerous because, for the most part, it is invisible money.
85. Generally, banks make more money from the consumers' use of debit cards over credit cards.
86. Debit cards are particularly popular among the group banks and other card issuers called "Generation P," for plastic. This group is composed of women and other consumers between ages 18 and 25.
87. Of the estimated $17.5 billion in overdraft fees that consumers pay to banks annually in the United States, nearly half are caused by debit card transactions and ATM withdrawals.

Chapter Fourteen: Franchising—Opportunities and Scams

88.   The Federal Trade Commission's (FTC's) "Franchise Rule," originally enacted in 1978, is the primary Federal law which governs franchising in the United States. The Rule requires franchisors (sellers of franchises) to provide potential franchisees (purchasers of franchises) with an extensive Franchise Disclosure Document (FDD) containing 23 specific items of information about the franchise offering, its officers and management, and other franchisees [www.ftc.gov]. Study this document carefully before joining or purchasing a franchise.

89.   Since the 1950s, "scamming" has had a long and rich history in the franchise industry.

90.   Do not join or purchase a franchise that does not require a due diligence investigation of the franchisor (seller of the franchise) by the potential franchisees (purchaser of the franchise).

91.   When considering the purchase of any franchise, make sure you have secured the services of a qualified attorney, competent accountant, and franchise expert to assist you.

Chapter Fifteen: Contract Law for the Consumer

92.   If you remember nothing else about contract law, remember this: When it comes to written or printed contracts, generally the BOLD (large) print giveth and the FINE (small) print taketh away.

93.   Even when a contract is not required to be written (pursuant to the Statute of Frauds or otherwise), it is a good idea for the parties or participants to have a written contract anyway; since it may be difficult to prove that an oral agreement existed, and there may remain questions regarding the terms of the agreement.

94.   In deciding whether a contract <u>must</u> be in writing, remember the Statute of Frauds mnemonic: "MY LEGS." (<u>M</u>arriage; one <u>Y</u>ear; <u>L</u>and; <u>E</u>xecutor; <u>G</u>oods; and <u>S</u>urety).

95. Federal and state laws require that all information and facts concerning a consumer contract transaction be fully disclosed to the consumer.

96. A number of state laws give consumers a legal right to cancel contracts in certain specific transactions within a relatively short time period after the consumer signs the contract. And, this cancellation can occur without the consumer giving the seller or other party a reason for the cancellation or even having to show "legal cause" [check with an attorney for legal advice on this issue and other topics related to this].

97. Four (4) particular contract clauses that the consumer should be aware of and review carefully are:

   (a) The Confessed Judgment Clause
   (b) The Arbitration Clause:
   (c) The Hold Harmless Clause; and
   (d) The Liquidated Damages Clause.

Chapter Sixteen: Secrets and Tips for Avoiding Debt Collection Harassment

98. Keep your debt problems in perspective. The worst a creditor generally can do to a consumer, other than repossession and foreclosure on property, is to (a) stop doing business with the consumer, (b)) file a legal action (lawsuit or arbitration) against the consumer, or (c) report the consumer's default to a credit bureau.

99. The consumer does have recourse against abusive and harassing debt collectors by way of Federal and state laws, and private legal action.

100. The definition for debt collector "abuse or harassment" is relatively and appropriately broad, and generally provides the consumer with several options ("The Eight (8)-Step Process") for relief.

101. Do not "over-promise" to the creditor or debt collector when discussing or negotiating payment or settlement of your debt.

102. Document everything when dealing with harassing and abusive creditors and debt collectors.

103. Four (4) names to remember and invoke when dealing with abusive and harassing creditors and debt (bill) collectors are:

    (a) The Federal Trade Commission;
    (b) The Attorney General's Office;
    (c) The Fair Debt Collection Practices Act (15 U.S.C. Section 1692); and
    (d) My Attorney.

104. There are at least thirteen (13) Federal benefits (sources of income) that are exempt from garnishment; with the exception that Federal benefits may be subject to garnishment under the following four (4) circumstances: (i) to pay delinquent taxes, (ii) alimony; (iii) child support, and (iv) student loans.

Chapter Seventeen: Recognizing and Avoiding Tax Debt Settlement Scams

105. In truth, what most so-called "tax debt settlement specialists" or companies are selling the tax client is just one (1) tax reduction strategy or process: the Offer in Compromise (OIC).

106. The average taxpayer's chances of getting the tax relief they want or expect from these alleged tax debt settlement "experts" is minimal or remote.

107. Beware of "over-promising" by the alleged tax debt settlement company. If the company's promises or marketing pitch to you sounds too good to be true, they probably are too good to be true. Some examples of "over-promising" by these firms include: "We can probably settle your tax debt for pennies on the dollar;" and "We should be able to get this process resolved for you immediately."

108. When judging or trying to decide the state or condition of the economy, I recommend the consumer look more at "Main Street" (his or her local economy) than "Wall Street", which is

certainly important but sometimes more remotely connected to the consumer's personal economic or financial condition.

Chapter Eighteen: Dealing with Government Agencies

109. Generally government agencies, like most large bureaucracies, operate a lot differently from you and I as individuals. Therefore, their actions can frequently not make a lot of sense to us as constituents and consumers. Be methodical, purposeful, and patient with them.

Chapter Nineteen: Avoiding Debtors' Prison In The United States

110. The United States technically abolished Federal imprisonment of debtors for unpaid debts in 1833.
111. Over 33 percent of all American states allow sanctions of incarceration against consumer borrowers who either cannot or will not pay their debts.
112. Almost universally within the United States, child support obligations and delinquencies are an exception to the "no debt collection by incarceration" practice.
113. Debtor arrests are usually couched or hidden in the format of creative nuances or instruments such as (i) violations of court orders, (ii) violations of probation or paroles; (iii) etc.

Chapter Twenty: Concluding Thoughts

114. You do not have to be nice when hanging up on unsolicited callers, especially commercial solicitors.
115. Most unsolicited offers are bogus or not worthy.

Other books by Charles Jerome Ware include:

"Understanding the Law: A Primer" (2008)

and

"The Immigration Paradox. 15 Tips for Winning
Immigration Cases" (2009)

WWW.CHARLESJEROMEWARE.COM

Charles Jerome Ware

http://charlesware.blogspot.com/

http://thelawyersmailbox.blogspot.com/

http://twitter.com/CharlesJWare

http://open.salon.com/blog/charlesjware